# THE EMPOWERING LEADER

How To Take Your Leadership
& Organization To The Next Level

JC HURTADO-PRATER

*How To Take Your Leadership &*
*Organization To The Next Level*

# THE EMPOWERING LEADER

## J.C. HURTADO-PRATER

Cannonball Publishing
San Diego, California

*To the men and women who have led me well; the men and women on whose shoulders I stand*

# CONTENTS

# ACKNOWLEDGEMENTS

For this book, I want to thank those leaders who I have deeply impacted my life and those people who have made me a better leader.

To Dr. Warren Bennis. We have never met, but you started a lifelong love and passion for the science and art of leadership. I am grateful to you for helping me find my "true north."

To Dr. John Maxwell. We have not met... yet. Yet, like many others, your influence has greatly influenced by understanding and practice of leadership. Thank you for giving your life away to so many,

To Dr. Todd Guy, Ritchie Walton and Todd Bell. From you I learned the importance of excellence and giving your best self to every task.

To Dr. David Jeremiah and Dr. Gary Bonner. From you I learned the importance of setting vision and recruiting others around a great vision. Dr. Jeremiah, from you learned the importance of discipline and focus in accomplishing personal and professional goals.

To Dr. Bob Brown. You have made a significant personal investment in my life and leadership. Thank you for your one-on-one mentorship and practical advice.

To Drill Sergeant Mercado. From you I learned the importance of leaders helping those whom they lead to raise their personal standards and reach their highest potential.

To Sergeant Mike Lane. From you I learned the importance of working until the job is done and always demanding the absolute best from myself and others.

To Nancy MacNamara. From you I learned the importance of being a true leader... tough when necessary but always fair and balanced.

To Dr. Russ Cox. From you I learned the importance of consistency. Every day getting up and getting after it... remaining focused and consistent on one purpose.

To the Shadow Mountain Hispanic Choir. I learned the value of empowerment from you. You helped me more than you will ever know. Thank you for allowing me to lead you while growing in my understanding of what true leadership is. I am eternally grateful to you.

To Kami Qualls, Monaca Price, Glynn Johnson, Joe Vargas and Jimmy Green. Each of you have helped make a better, more disciplined and more focused leader. I am still learning and growing. Thank you for your honest feedback along my journey.

To Nicole Pearson. For being an amazing friend, encourager and constant inspiration.

To Regan Reese. For being a solid rock in my story and for helping me understand the purpose and meaning of life. I am grateful for you.

# INTRODUCTION

Everything rises and falls on leadership.

These are the words of leadership guru John Maxwell. No words ring truer. Everything rises and falls on leadership. National and local governments rise – or fall – on leadership. Schools, colleges and universities rise – or fall – on leadership. Cities and communities rise – or fall – on leadership. For-profit and non-profit organizations rise – or fall on leadership. Religious institutions rise – or fall – on leadership. Families rise – or fall – on leadership. On a very personal level, your own life will rise – or fall – leadership.

Leadership is everything.

Yet, simply stating "leadership is everything" can only go so far.

Leadership, in and of itself, is more of an ethereal ideal. Part science, part art, but still something "out there." Leadership cannot simply happen. Leadership is a action word that happens only in concert with people. Books, while helpful, cannot lead. Systems, while important, cannot lead. Structures, while necessary, cannot lead. Courses, classes and seminars, while advantageous cannot lead.

Leadership can only happen within the context of person to person.

Therefore, when we say, everything rises and falls on leadership, what we are truly saying is, "Everything rises and falls on a person's capacity to lead others." In theory, leadership is a wonderful idea. Yet, in theory, leadership has very little power to get anything done. It takes people leading other people to accomplish a vision, mission or goal.

So, leadership is a very personal activity. It is an activity that refers to the capacity of a person in this leadership role.

Yet, it is important to understand capacity means nothing minus the willingness to learn and grow.

This is the point of this book, The Empowering Leader.

I believe most people have the capacity to lead greatly. Capacity is a fancy way to say "potential." Everyone has the potential within them to lead whomever and however they wish to lead. However, few will ever reach their full capacity to lead greatly.

Why?

Because leadership is a difficult task.

Empowering leadership is near impossible.

Leadership requires the science and the art of getting things done through other people. We think of the great generals of our past. The charismatic leader who stands in the front of thousands and, with flourish and dramatic speech, motivates the masses to action. This is the Great Man theory of leadership. Superman. Superwoman. Batman. Cat Woman. Spider-Man. Spider-Woman. Heroes and heroines who take on the hard task while others stand back, watch and take orders.

Having never been Superman, I cannot speak to the ease of this kind of leadership. However, this kind of leadership is a central-figure-focused leadership. The hard work of the leaders is focused on self. The leader must be great. The leader must have all the answers. The leader must be strong, physically and mentally. The leader must never be discouraged. The leader must never ask for help. Everything rises and falls on the leader. The world sits and waits in great anticipation for the what the leader will do.

This is not leadership. At least, not the kind of leadership we truly desire or value in today's economy.

14

Leadership today requires a much different kind of leader. Just as, within the field of education, we are witnessing the movement from the teacher-as-guru towards a teacher-as-guide model, in the field of leadership we are moving from the leader-as-guru towards a leader-as-guide model. In a conference I attended in recent years, business author and speaker Donald Miller shared with 3,000 leaders from across America the importance of leaders/teachers moving from expert to guide. He used examples from our favorite comic book heroes, such as the ones listed above, to showcase the changing landscape today where people no longer desire a hero in their lives. As a matter of fact, most people see *themselves* as the heroes in their own stories and journeys. Because of the fact that every story can only hold one hero, there is no room for you to be the hero for your people. That role is already taken.

What you can be – what your people want you to be – is a guide for them.

Think of every superhero that you know. If you were to put this book down and go watch the movies of every superhero, they would each something in common. This *something* is very important to the role and arch in the journey of the hero.

Each of the superheroes that we know and love have, we can call, a guide; someone they can call on when they are need of help. The guide is the person in whom the superhero finds their own strength and encouragement. In the moments when the superhero has faltered and must make a comeback, it is the guide who calls them back to action. Often, this guide is one of the most powerful characters in the life of any superhero.

This is the role of The Empowering Leader.

In recent years, the most famous buzzword has been Servant Leadership. While servant leadership is not a new term in history, as the philosophy of servant leadership is based on the writings and teachings of Lao Tzu, Chanakya, Cicero, Plutarch and the Bible, it was Robert Greenleaf who coined this term "The Servant as Leader" in the 1970's. The traits of servant leadership include the following: empathy, commitment to the growth and development of people, foresight, stewardship, listening, persuasion, building community, conceptualization and awareness.

While all of these traits are important in the life of any leader, I believe the term "servant leader" to be somewhat flawed.

In any organization, there must be a leader who casts the vision and those who implement the vision. Those who cast the vision are the leaders. Sure, great leaders will take input from those they lead – this is essential to leadership – but the leader must lead the organization. In addition, there are certain roles each person must fulfill within an organization.

Take the example of flying on an airplane. There are certain roles we expect the people who fly us around the world to take on. There is the person who books our flight, the person who takes our ticket and weighs our baggage, the person who loads our baggage on the plane, the person who checks our ticket at the gate, the person who explains the emergency procedures and brings us our drinks and, finally, there is the pilot. Each of these people have a role within the system of flying. Our collective preference is that each person sticks with their role within the system. Of course, we hope each of these people work well together, treat each other with respect and serve each other for the good of the system, but we would get a little worried if we looked out our window and saw the pilot loading our bags underneath the plane or filling the tank with fuel. It is safe to say, we want our pilots to place their focus on what they are greatest at...flying the plane.

The same should be with any healthy organization. Each person has a role to fill. There is the CEO and there is the person who cleans the restrooms at night. Each person is just as valuable to the organization but each person plays very different roles. I do not wish to see the CEO cleaning the restrooms at the end of the night just as I do not wish to see the night shift janitor calling the strategic shots for the organization.

Call me elitist but this is not how an organization is supposed to run.

I want the CEO and the janitor to know each other and get along but I do not care if the CEO is *serving* the janitor.

A better form of leadership – and better semantics – is empowerment.

Let's define empowerment

*Empowerment, as we will discuss in this book, is allowing each person within the organization to do what they do best in the way they do it best towards the aim of the organization.* This is empowerment. My hope is to convince you to believe empowering leadership as being a more effective style of leadership than both the Great Man theory of leadership and the Servant Leader theory of leadership. Both forms of leadership are good and necessary, yet both fall short of empowering leadership.

Learning is about change. My hope is that reading this book, you will not simply gain more head knowledge. My hope is that these words will be driven deep into your subconscious mind and that, in those areas where you need change, that you will experience great change. Even greater, I hope those around you will experience and benefit from this change. My hope is that the change that happens in you will be experienced across your company, your organization, your community and your family.

While this books is designed and written for the organizational leader, the principles will apply across every aspect of life. Leadership is interchangeable. A truly great – and Empowering Leader – does not need to be held to one field. Because leadership is about people and people exist in every industry, the leadership knowledge you gain in this book will be transferable across industries and communities.

Many years ago, Samuel Johnson stated these words: "The job of the teacher is the remind more than it is to instruct." This is a saying I repeat often in my talks and my writings. The role of this book is to simply serve as a helpful reminder to you. If you are reading this book, you are a leader. You may have some areas that need growth, just as we all do, but you are a leader. My role is to help you fine tune your leadership style and skills for the betterment of your people, your organization and your community.

Now, sit back, settle in and relax while we take a journey to help you reach your fullest capacity as you become a leader that others truly want to follow... an empowering leader.

# DEFINING EMPOWERMENT

Empowerment is allowing each person within the organization to do what they do best in the way they do it best towards the aim of the organization.

In its very basic form, empowerment is giving away power.

Nothing more. Nothing less. Giving away your empower to those who have shown they are capable of taking that power, growing it and helping to make the team more effective and successful.

Sound easy? Not so much.

This books details what it takes to truly give power away as you seek to become an effective and Empowering Leader. Before one can give away power, one must first have power. After one attains power, one must then attain the mindset and ability to give that power away.

I think of parenting.

When a child is in their younger years, all of the power rests within the parent or guardian. The child has no power because, in so many ways, the child is helpless. As the child grows and matures, the healthy parents slowly begins to release power. Bathing alone. Eating alone. Choosing their own clothes. Choosing the color of their bedroom. Picking out toys. Going to the mall with friends. Getting a driver's permit. Buying them a car. Allowing them to leave the house for days on end with friends. Sending them off to college. Walking them down the aisle. Moving them into their own place.

This is the process of empowerment. Slowly giving over freedom and power as the person earns more freedom and power. This is what a healthy parent does.

The unhealthy parent? They hold on to the power for as long as possible. Why? Fear of losing someone they love. Fear of losing control.

Empowering Leadership is much like great parenting. Slowing giving over power until the person working for you is in a position where they no longer need you.

This is not an easy process. Like everything, Empowering Leadership begins in the mind and flows through the actions of the Empowering Leader.

This book explains how.

# THE HEART OF AN EMPOWERING LEADER

Who are you?

Who are you really?

Before we can dive in further to what it means to be an empowering leader, you must start with understanding who you are. Leadership begins with self. You cannot lead others unless you can lead yourself. Correction: you cannot lead others – for the long haul – unless you can lead yourself.

We all know fakes and imposters. Leaders who have held very powerful positions, yet, over time, their leadership has not aged well. In fact, in this time period in which this book was written, we are witnessing men and women (primarily men) who have been leading teams and organizations for decades whose careers end up tailspinning in their later years. Their careers – built over many years – come to a screeching halt. Once powerful men are relegated to beach houses and courtrooms, their fame and power stripped because they lacked the heart of an empowering leader.

They were skillful. They were savvy. They were smart. All very important traits in leaders. However, they lacked character. They lacked a True North, a point of reference to inspire them forward. They were led by their whims and their emotions. Eventually they were outed. Their darker sides unearthed for all to see. They were cast aside. Rejected.

Once powerful. Today nothing.

We do not seek to become truly Empowering Leaders out of fear of what may happen to us should we fail. No, we seek to become Empowering Leaders because we have but one life to live. For those who are given the mantle of leadership, you understand how sacred it is to hold the lives of other people in your hands. To hold influence over communities, educational institutions, companies, organizations and families.

You desire to become an Empowering Leader because it is right and good. You desire to become an Empowering Leader because you desire to use your leadership to inspire others on towards greatness, to help those in your charge reach their full and highest potential. You desire to end your time on planet earth and have scores, even hundreds, of people line up to say of you, "He made me better." "I achieved because of her." This is what you desire.

Yet, this journey towards becoming an Empowering Leader starts with you.

It starts inside of you.

I have compiled a list of 3 traits you must find within your character in order to be a truly Empowering Leader. There are many foundational traits a leader can – and should – have. This chapter aims to focus on these three traits: Mastery, Integrity and Humility.

A leader's life must be marked by all three. On these traits, one cannot waiver. No exceptions can be made with these three traits. All three must be present in the life of a leader.

When a leader has mastery and integrity but no humility, they are arrogant...and therefore not empowering. When a leader has integrity and humility but no mastery, they are incompetent...and therefore not empowering. When a leader has humility and mastery but no integrity, they lack true confidence...and therefore are not empowering. The life of the empowering leader must be marked with Mastery, Integrity and Humility.

On an encouraging note, leadership is more science than art. Sure, there are some people who are just wired to lead. For the rest of us, we can learn. It will take time. It will take false starts. It will take disappointments. However, leadership is within the reach any person who desires to lead and is willing to put in the time and work in order to lead well.

Let's dive in.

# MASTERY

Mastery is key in the life of an empowering leader. Leaders must have mastery over themselves and their context in order lead others. By mastery, as you will see, we mean knowledge. The Empowering Leader never "masters" others and would feel uncomfortable in any role where he or she must be a master over others. Mastery refers to self. The ability to know oneself, one's strengths and weaknesses and to understand how these strengths and weaknesses influence decisions, choices and leadership.

Mastery does not mean a life lived with perfection. Just the opposite. Oftentimes, those who have truly mastered their lives are those who have gone to war with themselves. Possibly it is a series of mistakes and blunders that led to the pursuit of mastery in life. Mastery is about the journey. It is about taking every success – and every failure – and understanding how these successes and failures inform the present and the future.

In this section, we will examine five traits of the mastered life. These traits include a conquered mind, the knowledge and love of self, living courageously, being guided by habits and systems and living a focused life. When ones life is characterized by these traits, they will exhibit a life worthy of leadership.

It is important to note these traits will not happen overnight. Mastery is a life long process of spinning plates. At certain points along the journey, you will focus more attention on one or two plates more than others. At other points, you will focus on the other plates. So long as the plates remaining spinning, you are on your way.

Let's dive in.

## A CONQUERED MIND

Every man-made created structure begins in the mind. The chair you are sitting in. The walls that are surrounding you. The bed you sleep in at night. The car you drive to work. The television in your living room. The refrigerator in your kitchen. You get the idea.

Everything that has been created by man has first started in the mind.

This is an overwhelming fact that speaks to the testament of the power of the mind. The mind has the power to create or destroy. The mind has the power to construct or deconstruct. The mind is a weapon that can be used for good or for evil. The mind determines the fate and the destiny for all mankind.

Going deeper, the mind has the power to empower or disempower the human within which the mind resides. Many people fail to recognize the power of the mind and never reach their full and highest potential in life.

The Empowering Leader has a mind that has been fully conquered.

While most people mindlessly allow the mind to lead them, The Empowering Leader understands that he/she must lead their own mind. Within every person, there resides three entities. The person (your physical make up – what people see), the conscious mind (what you do) and the subconscious mind (what controls you – why you do what you do).

I have written extensively about the power of the mind in my two previous books and will probably continue to write on this subject as I grow in my understanding of the subject. One can never underestimate the power your mind has over you, your choices and the trajectory of your life. A leader... Correction... a *great* leader is one who has conquered their own mind.

What does this mean?

In order to understand this, let me briefly describe the three aspects to you.

### *Your Physical Presence*

This is part of you that everyone sees. Your face, your eyes, your hair... basically, how you present yourself to the world.

Your outer presence has no power to decide what you will or will not do in life. However, your outer presence is a direct reflection of what is happening within your mind. How you present yourself to the world is a direct reflection of what is happening on the inside, deep in the recesses of your mind. I do not mean your looks, although your looks are telling. It goes deeper than this. There are many people who look amazing on the outside, yet are struggling on the inside. No, what I mean is how you present yourself to the world... over the long haul.

As we talked about earlier, there are those leaders who have what I call "staying power." They are the leaders who have remained in their leadership position for years with no hint of scandal inappropriate behavior. These leaders are like fine wine; they get better with age. We do not hear about these leaders as often as we should.

What we do hear about – in the news and on social media – are the leaders who falter. The ones who resign or are fired because of mistakes they make at some point in their career. The most traumatic instances are when we hear of leaders who have been around for decades and, just as they are about to exit the leadership scene, scandal hits. In recent years, one of the most shocking cases of 4th quarter failure was Coach Joe Paterno, the decades-long coach of Penn State University. A revered coach and beloved figure at Penn State, his career came to a crashing end when it was revealed he helped to cover up sexual abuse allegations made against one of his assistant coaches. He died a broken-hearted man, his legacy forever tarnished, his statue removed from campus; a cautionary tale for leaders who lack character in any aspect of their lives.

The Empowering Leader has "staying power." He/she is able to be around for decades and retire on top because they have fully mastered their own mind and, therefore, have fully mastered their context. While every leader makes mistakes, nothing shocking is ever revealed about The Empowering Leader. There are no hidden corners. There are no surprises that would rock the evening news. There is nothing that will ever be revealed to the public that will cause the demise of this leader.

The physical presence – what you see – of the leader remains consistent for decades, even centuries.

Yet, again, this is because there is nothing hidden within the life of The Empowering Leader.

**25**

## Your Conscious Mind

Your conscious mind is what you do. The decisions you make on a daily basis make up your conscious mind.

What you eat. How you drive. Walking. Singing. Playing with your kids. Going to work. Exercising. Writing. Reading. All of these are conscious mind activities. Most of what you do throughout the day is a direct result of the workings of your conscious mind.

The good you do? Done in the conscious mind. The not-so-good you do? Also done in the conscious mind. Every action you take is the working of your conscious mind.

Most people remain right here during their life. They simply *do* without ever understanding why they do what they do. Most people in life remain stuck in some area of their life because they focus their attention on the conscious mind – what they do.

Take the example of losing weight. The diet industry is a multi-billion-dollar industry based on people living in their conscious. We get older, our metabolism slows, we exercise less and continue to eat the same kinds of food we ate in our teen years and, as a result, we gain weight. So, we go on a "diet" and have success for a few weeks only to gain back even more weight in the end. Why? We have not gone deeper on why we are gaining so much weight. Then, after "dieting" does not work, we decide to exercise even harder. We pay for a gym membership and sign up to run two marathons within the next six months. Within three weeks, we are back on the couch, putting off going to the gym "until tomorrow."

We have all been there.

Waging a war on ourselves by fighting small battles in the conscious mind when really the war must be won deep in the trenches of the subconscious mind. This is where the mind is fully conquered.

## Your Subconscious Mind

You are fully controlled by your subconscious mind. Your actions and what people see when you show up in a room is 100 percent based on the happenings in the deep recesses of your mind.

26

If you want to fully conquer your mind and master your context, the subconscious mind is where you will do it. And, once you know how to conquer your mind, you can accomplish almost everything you wish.

The subconscious mind is a deep mystery, but here is what we do know about your subconscious mind:
- Your subconscious wiring is formed between the ages of 1-10 based on what you saw, heard and experienced during that time period.
- Every decision you make is rooted in the subconscious mind.
- The subconscious mind can be re-wired through intentional, daily practice and changing your habits.

You want to know what controls the choices you make? You want to know where your limitations come from? You want to know where your deepest desires come from? You want to know why you cannot lose the weight you want to lose? You want to know why that person you love continues to make choices that are hurtful and disappointing? You want to know why your co-worker seems to have it all going for her when you cannot get a grip on life?

Look no further than the context, happenings or environment you – or they – experienced within the first 10 years of your life.

Was your home a loving and empowering environment? Did you experience abuse? What was playing on your television, computer or phone? What music did you listen to? Was your house messy or clean? Did you gain lots of affirmation or were you consistently being criticized? Were your parents your heroes or people you were afraid of? Were they even present? What food did you eat? What was celebrated in your early life? What has punished? What was your relationship like with your extended family? What brought you joy? What gave you anxiety?

Answering these questions – and more – based on your first 10 years of life will provide all the answers you need to know about the person you are today.

I think about the saying I have heard said many times to would-brides choosing a potential mate: "Look at how a young man treats his Mom. This is a direct reflection of how he will treat you." The same could be said to would-be husbands: "Look at the relationship a young lady has with her father; this will be a direct correlation to the relationship she will have with you." Why is this true? Imagine a young man who grew up with a very loving and empowering Mother. She adored him. She loved on him. She was a source of comfort and joy for him. He loved her deeply. He found her to be a safe and empowering person. His relationship with all women will reflect this relationship he had with his Mother. Now, picture the inverse. Another young man grew up with a mother who physically, verbally and emotionally abused him. Possibly she was abused by her own father and was projecting the anger she had towards her father onto her son. What will this young man's view of women be?

You get the idea. How we see the world – and the people in the world – is directly tied to our experiences when we were young.

When I look at many of the dynamic organizational leaders of our time, many of them grew up in loving and empowering homes with either a father or mother (or both) whom they could look to for guidance, protection and leadership. They had models to live by in their own parents and grandparents.

This upbringing between the ages of 1-10 guides the remainder of their life.

Anytime you look at someone and see success or failure, know you are looking at the consequences of the first ten years of their lives.

This is the power of the mind. Every decision you make is directly tied to the power of your subconscious mind.

### Conquering The Subconscious Mind

For most people, the destines of their lives are set in those early foundational years. This is why many communities face cycles of wealth or cycles of poverty. People live out what they learned in their early years. Communities are simply large groups of people who reside in the same context and are impacted by the same influences and surroundings.

On a personal level, I grew up in a trailer park. There was a oft-repeated saying that went like this this: "You can take the boy out of the trailer park, but you can't take the trailer park out of the boy."

There is some truth to this saying.

What you are in your early ears is often a direct reflection of what you will be when you get older... unless you reverse engineer your life.

Here is what I mean.

Let's say your first ten years of life were not great. You had an absent father and an angry mother. You grew up in a home where education was not valued. Your mother was emotionally abusive; you never knew who was walking into the front door every time she came home. You were fed Pop-Tarts and HotPockets as a regular part of your diet. Exercise was never emphasized in your home. No one ever looked at you said anything positive. You just existed.

In your early high school years, you cross paths with a very successful businessman. A man who has it all. A great partner, a great family, a beautiful home, nice cars and is in outstanding physical health. Something about this man strikes you and you decide you want to escape your life and become just like this person.

You do as much homework on this person as possible and discover he went to such-and-such school and majored in such-and-such subject. You study his life and career path. You find out that he works out in the gym every day, is a good husband to his wife and good father to his kids. He is also a wealthy person who own several cars, a boat and an airplane. He is living the life you have always dreamed of.

You make the decision to become just like this person.

Yet, it seems that every time you get going towards your goals, something stands in your way. You struggle with your studies. You have no motivation to work out at the gym. You cannot stand eating healthy food. You spend money as fast as it comes in saving very little, if anything. You find work but find yourself out of work due to a lack of work ethic. You even tell someone you want to be just like this person and they laugh at you. "You will never have that life!," they say to you.

You stare at this person and cannot figure out why you are not achieving the same success they are.

You have two options here: First, try to find out your mentor's upbringing. How were they raised? Who were their mentors? What was their home life like? What are their habits and systems? Model those habits and systems to a "T." Second, and this probably your best bet towards success, you can rewire – or reverse engineer, your own brain to become the person you want to become.

Modeling someone's behavior is a good thing. However, modeling will not help you fundamentally alter who you are in order to reach your goals. Rewiring your brain is the sure-fire way for you, over time, to radically shift your foundation in order to conquer your mind.

How do you rewire your brain? Change your inputs.

It's that simple.

Yet, not simple at all.

Here is how it works. The physical body takes action directed by the conscious mind which is directed by the subconscious mind. The subconscious mind is directed by the inputs from your early ages.

The subconscious mind has no ability to think for itself. It simply takes in information and wires your mind based on the inputs.

It's that simple.

In order to re-wire your subconscious mind, you must change your inputs.

What are you watching? Change it. What are you listening to? Change it. Who are you surrounded by? Change them. What is your current environment? Change it. I would go so far as to ask, "What are you eating?" Change it.

All of your inputs formed you and continue to shape the man/woman you are today. If you want to change who you are, change your habits, change your inputs, change your diet, change your context and change your friends.

This is where the challenge lies. Most people lack the courage it takes to make the necessary changes in their lives.

Most people like their current habits. Most people like their current inputs. Diet is one of the hardest aspects to change for most people. Most people feel comfortable within their context. Most people don't want to be alone and therefore do not want to change their associations and friends.

Therefore change never comes. The mind is never conquered. Full potential is never reached.

It is hard to change what already is. You will be fighting *you* in the process of changing you.

You will face massive amounts of anxiety as you push through your comfort zones and work to rewire (conquer) your mind. You will experience loneliness and confusion. There will be sadness and frustration as you forge a new path for your life. Your former self (your subconscious mind) will continue to pull you back to what is safe and comfortable for you (the foundation that was set for you during your earliest years.) There will be a constant war between the person you want to be and the person your subconscious mind believes you to be. You have to be ready for this daily battle against your former self.

This daily battle is what holds most people back. They lack the courage to go to war with themselves.

To some extent, everyone who desires success in life will fight this. Anyone who desires to be an Empowering Leader will fight the idealized version of themselves and the person they truly are. This is what conquering the mind is all about. Daily moving in the direction of your full and highest potential, sometimes against all odds.

It starts in the mind.

Change your habits. Change your inputs. Change your diet. If necessary, change your context and your friends.

Get the necessary help you need in this stage. Get counseling. Get coaching. Find someone who believes in you and seek their help as you move towards the highest version of yourself.

The Empowering Leader is one who has fully conquered his/her mind and daily is able to move past resistance.

## KNOWS SELF. LOVES SELF.

Because of the importance of the mind, we spent a great deal of time there. For every would-be empowering leader, true empowerment begins in the mind. This is where the battle starts. Conquering the mind.

The conquered mind is truly knowledge of self. One who has conquered their mind is one who fully understands their mind and knows how their mind will cause them to make decisions and choices in life.

Normally, when we hear the term "conquered" we tend to think of destruction. When an army conquers a city, it completely overtakes and destroys the city, murdering its inhabitants and taking from the land what they want.

This is not fully what we mean when we say "conquering the mind." Yes, there is an element to overtaking your mind. However, one cannot destroy the mind. Even those deepest thoughts and memories you carry around cannot truly be destroyed. You can destroy habits – and we will discuss this further later in this chapter – but you cannot destroy your mind.

However, while cannot actually destroy your mind, you can do the second most powerful thing: You can know your mind.

By knowing your mind, you can know your self.

To know yourself is to understand yourself. Who you are. Why you are the way you are. Where you came from. Your purpose. Your vision. Your mission. Your values. Your principles. To know and understand why you do what you do.

We will refer to this as your Personal Constitution.

Your Personal Constitution is the reason you exist and what you most care about all written in a document for you to reference on a consistent, if not daily, basis. Your Personal Constitution will consist of five sections detailing your Purpose, Vision, Mission, Values and Principles. I recommend you have this Personal Constitution written down and placed strategically in areas where you will review it often.

Why do you exist? This is your purpose.

Where is your life going? This is your vision.

How will you get to where you are going? This is your mission.

What are the words you want to describe your life? These are your values.

What are the rules that guide your choices and decision? These are your principles.

Once you can answer these questions – once you know your Personal Constitution – you will have a great understanding of you who are.

Once you know your Personal Constitution, write it down. Review it often. Your Personal Constitution and personal mastery are one and the same.

Personal mastery comes from knowing the answers to these questions purpose, vision and mission and aiming every moment of your life towards these answers. Most importantly, personal mastery is working to overcome the obstacles that will inevitably stand in your way as you pursue your purpose, vision, and mission according to your values and principles. We talked about this in the previous section where we discussed the power of your mind. You will counter obstacles as your mind works overtime to keep you safe within your comfort zone (the foundation you gained between the ages of 1-10). Mastery comes from understanding how your mind works and to remain working towards your purpose, vision and mission.

This is to know oneself.

Yet, knowing oneself is simply the starting point. To reach the highest levels of mastery, one must love themselves. By this I mean, one must fully accept the full makeup of who they are.

Love and acceptance of self is the starting point for leadership.

There are many men and women who are in leadership roles and should not be, but rather find themselves there on a quest to prove themselves. They lacked the proper love from one or both parents, were victims of bullying at an early age or have a "chip" on their shoulder. They are not true leaders in the sense of the word "leadership."

Leadership is about expressing oneself rather than proving oneself.

When a person engages in proving him or herself, they are not living authentically who they are. I speak a great deal about this subject of love and acceptance of self in my books because this is vastly important for would-be leaders to fully realize and understand.

Life (or God) has given you everything you need to succeed, thrive and live a life that adds value to those around you, your community and the planet. A lack of acceptance is your way of telling Life (or God) that you reject the gifts and personality you have been given. You then decide to become someone else...some you feel will bring you the sense of fulfillment you have always longed for.
Yet, in this process you are only fooling yourself. You may fool others, but not for long. The reality is that everyone around you can see you for exactly who you are. They see your talents. They see your gifts. They see your potential, or lack of it. When you work to be someone you are not, you will eventually be found out for who you really are. Sadly, in this process, you could lose months – even years – of your life trying to live a life you were never meant to live.

A mastered life – the life of an empowering leader – is a person who fully loves, accepts and embraces every aspect to who they are. They live by their Personal Constitution. They focus on their strengths. They are inner driven. Life becomes about expressing what is on the inside rather than proving themselves to the world.

Take a moment and think of the greatest leaders you know. Try and think of three different people. What is the one thing they all have in common?

Every single one of them were living fully expressed lives. By fully expressed I mean that these leaders were not aspiring to be great leaders. They were simply living their own purposes, visions and missions according to their own authentic values and principles. These are people who know who they are, why they exist and fully embrace their gifts and personalities.

True leadership must from a deep and authentic place within the life of the leader.

Mastery of self is knowing, loving, accepting and embracing oneself.

## LIVES COURAGEOUSLY

Once you know your purpose, vision, mission, values and principles, your Personal Constitution, it takes courage to live it out.

Because the aspects of one's Personal Constitution are rarely found within a person's comfort zone, it takes courageous living to consistently step out of one's comfort zone and live a fully mastered life.

Nothing about the living a fully mastered life is easy. It is not easy to discover one's Personal Constitution. For many people, this process takes years and a breadth of experiences to fully understand. For some, there is a struggle that happens in coming to love and embrace who they are.

Once a person has wrestled with their life and has become settled on their Personal Constitution, the real work begins... living it out.

First, when living your Personal Constitution, you must refer to it daily. Every day, you must wake up and remind yourself why you exist, where you are going, how you intend to get there, what matters most to you and the rules that will govern your life. If you do not take this step on daily – or weekly – basis, the demands of life will determine your Personal Constitution. The pressures of ever day will determine where you end up. You must have the discipline to daily remind yourself of why you exist.

Second, you must admit to the fears you will face on a daily basis as you live out your Personal Constitution. Living a fully mastered life will be hard and will cause an unknown amount of fear and anxiety. This fear and anxiety will be different for different people but it will exist. It is important to acknowledge these fears and accept that they do exist.

Third, you must be willing to face these fears and move through them. There is no way to move around the fears. Moving around the fears is the cause of depression, addiction and lack of confidence for many people. They see the goal. They see where they need to be. They encounter fear. They turn back or try to find a shortcut. There is no shortcut. Avoiding fear relegates you to a life of mediocrity. Fear cannot be avoided if you are to live your Personal Constitution. You must do the actions you are most afraid of. This is the only way to move past fear; by moving through it. This takes courage.

Fourth, the courageous life requires remaining positive in the face of negativity and personal resistance. It may seem cruel, but there are forces that will work to keep you from living your Personal Constitution. Very few people have a vested interest in your success. At times, it may feel you have little vested interest in your own success. In the midst of the resistance you will feel – outward and inner – you must remain positive, grateful and upbeat. You must not let the negative influences that exist – news, media, friendships, co-workers, relationships – to cause you to move towards negativity. In order to keep out these influences, you will be required to say "No." No to certain inputs and certain relationships. Doing this takes courage.

The mastered life – the life of the empowering leader – is a courageous life that works to keep pressing forward towards living one's Personal Constitution. No matter the roadblocks. No matter the obstacles. No matter the outer context. To keep pushing forward until the goal has been reached.

This is courage.

## GUIDED BY HABITS AND SYSTEMS

The Personal Constitution is key to a mastered life. Understanding your purpose, vision, mission, values and principles is foundational on your journey to becoming a empowering leader.

Yet, knowing your Personal Constitution and *living* your personal constitution are two very different things. Just like the knowing the law and living the law are two very different things. You may mentally *know* the speed limit in your city, but *following* the speed limit is a different thing altogether. If you have ever been pulled for driving too fast you know that the officer who hands you the ticket could care less if you *knew* what the speed limit was. He is giving you a ticket because you knew the speed limit and *chose* not to follow the speed limit.

The same can be said for you Personal Constitution on your road to mastery. This Personal Constitution has the ability to change the trajectory of you life, but you must have make the daily choice to follow your constitution.

How?

By creating habits and systems that guide your life.

Habits are actions you choose to take that will help you reach your goals. Systems are a series of actions, or habits, you design into your life that you believe will help you reach your goal.

Let's say you want to lose 10 pounds. Many people can relate this kind of a goal. It's the New Year or you have an event coming up on your calendar and you have a certain way you want to look or feel.

What do most people do? They set the goal, feverishly work out, radically change their diet and give themselves a deadline to lose the desired weight.

How often does this work? Rarely.

Why? Because the achievement you are seeking is goal-based rather than being based on habits and systems.

Living with systems and habits require a lifestyle change over a long period of time. This idea of change over a long period of time is hard for most people. We want results today...right now. Yet, living by goals rarely achieves long-term results.

A better way to lose 10 pounds is to transform your lifestyle so you can keep the weight off long-term. This requires better habits and systems.

For example, you may decide on the following habits: (1) exercise for 1 hour every day, (2) lift weights 4 days a week, (3) do cardio 3 days a week, (4) eat only protein for breakfast and lunch while limiting yourself to healthy and natural carbs at dinner, (5) get 7 hours of sleep every night and (6) drink 3 liters of water a day to remain hydrated. These are all habits... and good ones I might add!

The system you put in place will determine your success in accomplishing those habits on a daily basis. With the goal, or outcome, you have in mind, your system might look like this:

- 5am – Wake up & Hydrate (every day)

- 6am – Work out (every day)
- 7am – Eat a protein-based breakfast and hydrate (every day)
- 12pm – Eat a protein-based lunch and hydrate (every day)
- 5pm – Eat a protein-based dinner with healthy carbs (every day)
- 7pm – Hydrate
- 10pm – Be in bed ready to fall asleep (every day)

This is a system you have put in place to help you achieve your outcome long-term. However, your focus moves from the goal/outcome to your habits and systems. You grade your success on how well you follow your habits and systems and, within time, the goal/outcome will be realized. By this time, however, you have changed your lifestyle as opposed to chasing some an elusive goal.

This is the mastered life. To focus on lifestyle systems and daily habits as opposed to momentary changes.

This means you hydrate even when you do not want to. Why? Your system demands it. You workout even on days when you are tired. Why? Your system demands it. You eat a protein-based diet even when you are surrounded by people who down unhealthy carbohydrates. Why? Your system demands it. You go to bed on time every night. Why? Your system demands this.

This is the power we have as human beings. We can make the choice to become exactly the person we want when we are brave enough to implement powerful systems in our lives that will help us reach ours goals.

They have a word to describe a person whose life is guided by systems and habits: Consistent.

Consistency is one of the most crucial traits for any leader.

People want to follow a person they can trust. A person who never wavers. A person who remains steadfast, even when all around them the world is crumbling. A person who shows up every time. A person whose actions match up with their words. These are foundational characteristics for an empowering leader.

These outward actions start with an inner commitment to living according to habits and systems.

Human beings are a mix of mind and emotions. The mind wants one things, the emotions want something completely different. Remember our discussion about the mind? Your conscious mind wants one thing. Your subconscious mind desires something different altogether. Usually your conscious mind is pointing you in the right direction while your subconscious mind is controlling your emotions. You know and understand the danger of living life based on your emotions. Most decision based on pure emotions turn out be disastrous for all involved, especially when a leader decides to base decisions on emotions.

Living a life based on systems and habits requires understanding one's Personal Constitution and living life according pre-stablished systems for success.

At times along the journey, you may need to change your systems and habits in order for you to attain the results and outcomes you are seeking. This is good thing. However, once you have settled on your systems and habits – and they are bringing you the success you desire – your only job is to maintain your systems and habits. Nothing will move you from these.

This is mastery.

## A FOCUSED LIFE

The conquered mind. Knowledge and love of self. Courageous living. A life directed by systems. These are all important aspects to the mastered life.

Yet, the final piece might be one of the most important ingredients.

Focus.

The ability to know your Personal Constitution and to live that constitution every day in spite of the many distractions that will inevitably come your way...this is focus.

As the famous inventor and entrepreneur Steve Jobs once stated, "Focus is about saying, 'No.'"

Unfortunately, what keeps most people from achieving their dreams and goals is not necessarily lack of opportunity in life. What keeps most people from reaching their highest potential is too much opportunity. The more talented and marketable you become, the more opportunities will come your way. Many of these opportunities will be inviting and exciting, new ways for you to expand your horizon. Because you are somebody working to reach your highest potential, you will be tempted to take every opportunity that comes your way. In the beginning of your leadership journey, this is well and good. You should try as many things as possible in order to know where your talents and gifts exist. Yet, the further you move through life, the more you will come to understand the power of focus in reaching your highest potential as a person and as a leader.

You have probably heard the term, "jack of all trades, master of none." Often people refer to themselves in this way as a means of joking. The reality is far more sad and disappointing. The danger of the unfocused life is reaching the end of your life and never having fully mastered anything. You may have many wonderful memories and photographs, yet you failed to reach your highest potential because you did not go deep on any one thing.

Focus is hard. The consequence of a life of focus is missing out...and missing out on many really great things. Jobs. Relationships. Opportunities.

Think about a long-term marriage. A marriage that lasts 50, 60 or 70 years. The reason the marriage stood the test of time has everything to do with the power of focus. Forsaking all others. Remaining married through the good times and hard times. Through sickness and health. Forgiving each other when it most difficult. Choosing to remain when it would be far easier to leave.

Marriages and relationships that last are built on the power of focus, even if unintentionally. Both parties have made the commitment to remain in the relationship based on an inner commitment to each other.

The focused life is a commitment you make with yourself to stay the course, no matter how painful it may be. To trust your intuition. To trust your Personal Constitution. To pursue your purpose, vision and mission no matter what life throws at you.

This is focus. This is mastery.

Trust is built when followers see a leader who remains focused in one direction for a long period of time. People want to follow a stable leader. Focus and commitment create stability. Stability develops in people the empowerment to grow, expand, fail, try again and pursue their own mastery.

The truly empowering leader is a stable, consistent and committed leader. Committed to the organization and committed to its people.

Know your Personal Constitution. Focus your life on it. Remove any distractions, obstacles or barriers that keep you from giving everything you need towards your Constitution.

Conquer your mind daily. Know, understand and love yourself daily. Live courageously daily. Be guided by your systems daily. Focus your life daily.

In this way you will live the mastered life. You are ready to lead others only when you are ready to lead yourself.

# INTEGRITY

To be who you say you are; that takes cleverness.

To be exactly who you are; this takes courage.

To live with integrity has nothing to do with morality, although it can. No, to live a life of integrity simply means who are exactly who you are.

In private, you are who you are. In public, you are who you are. On the platform, you are who you are. In the dressing room, you are who you are.

Simply put, you are who you are. Consistently.

Who are you? That is for you to decide. Whoever this person is, this is who you must be.

You do not like the person you are? You cannot live with absolute integrity because it will cause you embarrassment?

Then change.

Go back and read the previous section and bring change to who you are.

We have all read about embarrassing resignations and firings of prominent leaders in every field; politics, religion, education, entertainment and many others. In each of these cases, the downfall happened for one reason: the image the leader portrayed in public and the person they were in private did not line up.

The empowering leader is authentic and transparent with who they are. They are open with their strengths and their weaknesses. There are no secrets.

Does this mean you, as a leader, need to share everything about your life? Absolutely not. Boundaries are important. Boundaries are necessary.

However, you are not fake. You do not have to wear masks for different situations you find yourself in. You can be your authentic self anytime, anywhere.

Why is integrity so important?
Integrity builds trust. When people know you, they can trust you. When people don't know you or are unsure that you are who you say you are, they cannot trust you. Sure, trust always takes time. However, trusts takes time and integrity. When people see you living authentically over a period of time they can trust that you are who you say you are.

But I cannot stress this enough... integrity is not a faith or moral issue. Integrity is simply being who you are. I would trust a thief who lived with integrity more than I would a religious man who said one thing and did another. With the thief, I know who I am talking to. I know what is standing in front of me. I know that I need to hold onto my wallet! With the religious man who espouses certain values yet lives another way, I do not know what I am getting. I hear him say one thing yet watch him do another. That cannot be trusted.

Integrity is simply being who you are. Consistently.

Live with integrity. Always.

# HUMILITY

Mastery.

Integrity.

These traits are nothing without humility. To master who you are and have the courage to be who you are only brings pride, the unhealthy form.

At its best, pride brings confidence to your life. At its worst, pride brings superiority, judgement, even hatred, towards others.

Humility is the secret ingredient to the heart of an empowering leader. Humility is the character trait that consistently reminds the leader that life and leadership is never about him or her.

Humility is not thinking less of yourself, it is thinking of yourself less.

This might be the greatest definition of humility.

Life is not about you. Life is about others. Life is about purpose. Life is about vision. Life is about mission. Life is about using your gifts and talents to empower and add value to others.

Life is not about you. The humble person understands this.

When faced with a courageous decision, the humble person is able to walk forward bravely because he or she understands the purpose, goal or vision is not about him or her.

What character traits or actions hold back most leaders?

Fear. Insecurity. Pride. Power grabbing. Taking advantage of others. Hubris. Greed.

At the root of all of these traits and actions is the unhealthy focus on self, even if unconsciously.

Fear always comes from a personal fear of the unknown, not wanting to venture into a new challenge.

Insecurity is rooted in the personal fear of losing someone or something.

Pride comes from a bloated view of self.

Power grabbing is rooted in insecurity which is rooted in the fear of losing someone or something.

Taking advantage of others comes from a bloated view of self combined with a personal emptiness.

Hubris is rooted in a bloated sense of self combined with the inability to take feedback from others.

Greed comes from a desire to hoard as much as possible due to a personal emptiness and fear of losing something valuable.

As you can see, each of these actions is rooted in SELF. A preoccupation with SELF.

I once heard a religious leader state that most leaders are taken down by three things: Money, Power or Sex. Is there anything fundamentally wrong with Money, Power or Sex? Not in the least. All three are good and necessary...when approached with humility.

The humble person approaches money with the understanding that the money he or she gains is a responsibility to the greater good. The humble person approaches power with the mindset of lifting up others and doing greater good in society. The humble person approaches sex as an act of giving.

For those who truly desire to be an empowering leader, longevity is a key component to being a great leader. Longevity only comes through humility.

You may be charismatic. You may be brave. You may be able to lead armies or corporations.

However, you will not remain in a leadership position for an extended amount of time without humility.

Humility is foundational for the heart of the empowering leader.

The question you may be asking is this, "How will I know when my life is characterized by humility?"

Here is the simple answer: When your purpose in life is to add value to others and you spend the balance of your days pursuing this purpose, your life is characterized by humility.

Adding value to others is not dependent on your career. You can add value in any profession.

Adding value to others is not dependent on how much money you have. You can add value to others with a smile or an encouraging word.

Adding value to others is not dependent on your status. Human beings are human beings. You can add value to others no matter your status in life.

No matter where life has you currently, you can always add values to others. You can be rich and add value to others. You can be poor and add value to others. No matter where you are in life, you can always add value to others.

When you are consistently adding value to others, you are living a life of humility.

# IMPORTANT TAKEAWAYS

- To have the heart of an Empowering Leader, your daily life must be characterized by Mastery, Integrity and Humility.
- Mastery has everything to do with understanding the power of your subconscious mind.
- Stop focusing on your goals. Set goals and the focus all of your energy on systems and habits.
- Focus is about making commitments to yourself and forsaking anything that keeps you from your personal commitments. Focusing is about saying "No."
- Integrity simply means to be who you are. If you do not like who you are, change who you are. Be authentic always.
- A life of humility is characterized by consistently adding value to others. Life is not about you.

# THE MIND OF THE EMPOWERING LEADER

We have talked about the Heart of the Empowering Leader. We now move from the Heart to the Mind.

As we talked about in the previous chapter, the mind truly controls everything. If you want to change your life, you must change your mind.

So, why did we place the mind in the context of the "Heart" of the Empowering Leader as opposed to the Mindset of the Empowering Leader.

The heart is foundational. The heart is your values, motives and Personal Constitution. In order to understand your heart, you must first understand your mind and what lies in those deepest recesses of your mind. Only then can you understand your heart.

When we talk about the mindset of a the empowering leader, we are talking about *how* you think as opposed to *why* you think what you think. Your beliefs and values affect why you believe what you believe. These beliefs are foundational; they are central to who you are as a person. To change these core belief can take lots of hard, intentional work and many years.

Changing *how* you think is different. We are now working within the conscious mind. In order to change the conscious mind, you simply need to speak what you intend to believe.

**47**

I do not know where you are on your journey towards becoming an Empowering Leader. Yet, having worked with many leaders and having been on my own leadership journey, I know the difficulty of being an Empowering Leader. Leadership is one thing. Empowering leadership is another thing altogether. Empowering leaderships gives power away. The Empowering Leader is the leader who seeks to work him or herself out of a job, so to speak.

The very act of giving away power is difficult. It is in human nature to hold on to power; to keep power to oneself out of fear. The empowering leader consistently examines those people who surround him or her and seeks to help these people reach their full and highest potential.

In order to be the kind of leader who gives away power to others, the Empowering Leader must have the following five mindsets: Love, Openness, Systems-Thinking, Purpose/Vision and Coaching.

# MINDSET OF LOVE

Leadership and love. Can the two mix?

Yes. Absolutely.

Hundreds of years ago Catholic theologian Saint Augustine stated these words, "Love is seeking the highest good for the other."

Often when we think about love, we think about something emotional or soft. In reality, actual love is much more logical and practical. We can feel emotions but often these emotions are not translated into action. Love, true love, is an internal commitment to seek the highest good for others and then to act on this commitment. In any interaction, we must ask ourselves, "What is best for the other person?" Asking this question is important as, more often than not, we are subconsciously asking, "What is best for me?" To think in the way of love takes a new approach. Yet, this new way of thinking is foundational for the empowering leader.

Now, I must say this: The purpose, vision and mission for the community, organization, family, team or project must always come first. Leadership is not giving into every whim of the people one leads. However, within the boundaries of the purpose, vision and mission, the leader must be able to look at those he or she leads and ask the question, "What is the highest good for this person?"

This idea of love can – and should – also be placed towards the community, organization, family, team or project you are leading. The idea is to always be asking, "What is best for others?"

Asking this question is important in times of conflict or in those moments when the leader's emotions are potentially clouding one's judgment. In those moments, it is important for the leader to stand back and ask the questions, "What is best for the whole? What is best for the person?"

This is a mindset of love. Taking the attention off self and placing that attention towards purpose, vision, mission and people.

You may be asking, "If I am always seeking the best for others, who is going to look out for me?"

This is the reality of leadership and why you must be careful before choosing to take on the responsibility of leadership. Leadership is never about you. Never. Leadership is always about purpose, vision, mission and others. Always.

Who takes care of you? You do.

This is another topic altogether, but it is your responsibility to care for you. It is your responsibility to find those things that empower you and to do those things.

When it comes to empowering leadership, it is always about others.

# MINDSET OF OPENNESS

Leaders must remain focused on the purpose, vision and mission. In addition, the job of the leader is to keep the team they are leading – no matter how large or small – focused on the purpose, vision and mission. However, within this rigid focus there must openness.

A mindset of openness comes back to this idea of humility that we spoke about earlier. The humble leader understands that he or she does not have all of the answers. The leader's primary job is to remain laser-focused on the purpose, vision and mission for the organization and to hire the very best person to help him or her accomplish the purpose, vision and mission. I would go even further and say the leader's job is to hire experts and to simply empower them (give away power.)

Hiring experts and allowing them run the organization is key.

Your job as the leader to simply make sure these experts have everything they need in order to succeed and then give them the freedom to do their jobs.

Leading experts requires that the leader must listen to these experts. The leader must make decisions – towards the purpose, vision and mission – based on the recommendations of the experts he or she hires.

I cannot stress this point enough.

The leader must make decisions – towards the purpose, vision and mission – based on the recommendations of the experts he or she hires.

Many leaders get themselves in trouble because they hire people and expect them to simply be "Yes" men and women. They hire people to simply do what they (the leader) want them to do. They hire experts and then micromanage them. In return, they lose them.

The mindset of openness means you shift how you see yourself as a leader. Again, your job is to hire the very best people, to resource them and keep them focused towards the purpose, vision and mission of the organization. We will talk about this mindset shift in the next section.

Openness requires flexibility, asking great questions, inviting feedback, listening and making decisions based on what your experts are telling you.

Choose to see your employees as experts or consultants. You have hired these experts to help you reach the mission. If you are a great leader, these experts will do the work for you...and happily do so.

Hire great people. Listen to them. And give these people the freedom and empowerment towards the purpose, vision and mission.

# MINDSET OF SYSTEMS THINKING

Systems thinking is taking a holistic approach to whatever it is you may leading...a community, organization, family, team or project.

A holistic approach require that you look at the entity you are leading from a birds eye view when making decisions about almost anything. A holistic approach values the entire system when looking at the success, or failure, of a project.

How is "systems thinking" empowering?

Systems thinking is empowering in that reward – or blame – is never placed on one individual. Rather, when there is success or failure, leaders understand they need to look at the entire system when judging the causes.

Let's use an example.

Bob's Cars is a used car dealership somewhere outside of a large and metropolitan city. For years, Bob's Cars have sold good used cars and have built a great reputation within the local community. However, Bob, the owner of Bob's Cars, has recently seen a slow and steady drop in business. As more new car dealers with bigger names – and more money – begin to saturate the local market, Bob needs to think about how to grow and scale his business. There are two approaches Bob can take. He can use Fragmented Thinking or Systems Thinking.

Fragmented thinking means that the Bob begins looking at different elements of the business and makes statements such as, "If we just do more marketing, we will grow!" Or, "If our salespeople just make more sales, we will grow!" Or, "If our advertising looked better, we would grow!" Or, "If our service department would get better, we would grow!" Now, all of these reasons may be correct, but this kind of thinking will be frustrating for Bob and, soon, for his employees.

When Bob begins thinking in fragments, he will start focusing his attention on individual parts of the business as opposed to the whole. If Bob decides the reason for the loss of business has to do with marketing, he will begin to micromanage the marketing department in order to get more effective production from this team. Possibly this is what the marketing team needs. However, more than likely they are doing the best they can with the tools they have. This micromanaging will only serve to frustrate the employees within this department, possibly causing some of them to leave the organization. They rightly will begin to believe they are being blamed for the slow decline of the business. In addition, they will feel the weight of the company to get sales back where it needs to go.

A better way to look at this issues is through the mindset of systems thinking.

If Bob were to take on the mindset of systems thinking, he might begin by asking the following questions:

- What is the national climate towards business right now?
- What is the national climate towards used car dealerships?
- On a national scale, what kinds of cars are people purchasing right now?
- On a more regional scale, what kinds of cars are people buying right now?
- Regionally, what is the business climate?
- Within the local community, what changes are taking place?
- Within the local community, what kinds of cars are people purchasing?
- With so many new dealerships moving in, what is a segment of the population that is being forgotten? How can I cater to this market?
- Are there new marketing techniques I am not using?
- Are there new sales techniques I need to train my staff on?
- What about the location of my business? Is my building and my lot appealing to customers?
- What are the major dealerships doing to attract business? Can we model our business after them?

If Bob is a great leader, he would bring his leadership team into the conversation, possibly through a weekend retreat. He would share reality with the leadership team and work with the team to take a bird's eye view of Bob's Cars. As a team, they would begin to look at their smaller system within the context of the larger system. They might even compare and contrast their dealership to another thriving used car dealership within the region or within a community that resembles their own community.

In this process of systems thinking, the leaders would look at their company with a very critical view, looking at any and every error within the system. They would look at their model organization and work to see how they change aspects with their system to resemble the model system.

From this discussion, the team would make recommendations on systems-wide changes to begin to implement.

In this way of thinking, there is no blame given to any one person. If there is a failing person, a systems-minded leader would ask the question, "How did the system fail this person?" The answer could simply be that the system hired the wrong person. In this case, the leaders would need to look at the system and ask how such a person was able to be hired. More than likely, there would need to be a systems change to the hiring process in order to make sure every hire is a good hire.

People are rarely, if ever, to blame within a systems-minded organization. Additionally, systems-minded leaders never put the blame on people. Again, if there is a challenging team member, the leader asks, "How did the system create this challenge?" Or, "What must I do different, as a leader, to help this person succeed?"

The success or failure of the organization rises solely on the system. The success or failure of the system rises solely on the leader who created the system.

Everything rises and falls on leadership. Everything.

# MINDSET OF PURPOSE AND VISION

Leadership is remaining on purpose, setting vision and empowering your community/organization/family/team to move the mission forward. You, as the leader must remain solely focused on the purpose and vision for the organization. This may be tough to hear, but the mission of your organization has little to do with you.

What?

I can feel you bucking that last statement. "Leadership is all about mission! What is a leader without a mission? Not a leader!"

Imagine telling a military general or CEO or hospital administrator or educational leader to leave the mission alone?

This is exactly what I am telling you to do.

Leave the mission alone.

Remember our definition of empowerment? Giving power away.

Let me explain using what I call the Cannonball Leadership Matrix. (Cannonball after the name of the of the consulting firm I own and operate.)

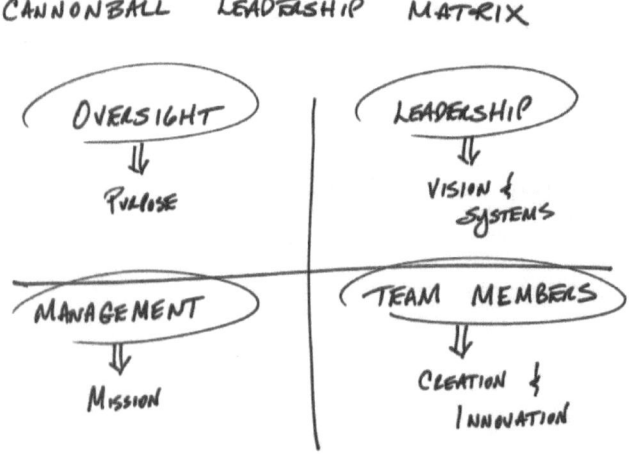

As you can see the leadership matrix is divided up into 4 different areas: Purpose, Vision/Systems, Mission and Creation/Innovation.

In most organization, you will be able to divide the organization into 4 distinct areas: Oversight, Leadership, Management and Team Members. Oversight is usually provided by a board of directors. Leadership of the organization is provided by the senior leadership team. Management of the organization is provided by the management team. The work of the organization is provided by the team members.

Let's go even deeper and correlate the Leadership Matrix with the roles within the organization:

- The job of of the Board of Directors is to provide Oversight to the organization to ensure the organization remains on its Purpose. Whatever the stated purpose for the organization, the job of the board is to ensure the organization remains within that stated purpose.
- The jobs of the Leadership Team is provide leadership for the organization by focusing on the Vision and Systems for the organization. The senior leaders focus their attention outwards and on the system as a whole. They are tasked with remaining laser-focused on the vision by consistently asking the questions: Where are we going? Are we heading in the right direction? What are the global trends within our industry? Are we prepared to face these trends head on? What are our competitors doing? Are we remaining competitive within our industry? What must we change in order to gain the competitive edge? In addition, the senior leaders remain laser-focused on the system of the organization, consistently working to change and improve the system where and when needed.
- The job of the Management Team is to "enforce" the Mission while creating an empowering culture for the employees of the organization. While the leadership team must remain focused on where the organization is going, the management team must be focused on the day-to-day "how." This is the nuts and bolts of how the organization runs. It's process. It's structure. It's people. The management team helps move the

mission forward by managing the forward movement of the organization.

- The job of the Team Members is to Innovate and Create. This is where the magic happens. This level is where the work of the organization takes place. Because the purpose of the organization is governed by the board, the vision and system of the organization is governed by the leadership team and the mission of organization is overseen by the management team, the team members are free to create and innovate without being encumbered by the minutiae of running the organization.

So you see what I mean when I say, "Leave the mission alone." The job the of the Empowering Leader is to remain focused on the vision for the organization and how to constantly improve the system so the management team and employees are able to complete the work they have been hired to do.

This is hard to do, especially within a smaller organization. While micromanaging can – and does – happen within organizations of all sizes, it is more prone to happen within a smaller organization where the leader feels that he or she must be involved in every aspect, every detail. Yet, the Empowering Leader is very intentional about hiring the right people and giving them the freedom and latitude to do what they need to do, be it manage the system or create and innovate. The Empowering Leader understands that when he or she takes the mantle of leadership, there are aspects of the organization they must give up. The primary job of the leader is not to manage but to empower great managers. The primary job of the leader is not to create and innovate but to empower his or her managers to empower their team members to create and innovate.

Hands off.

Remain focused on the vision of the organization. Remain focused on the system of the organization.

This is the sacrifice of leadership. You no longer get to do the work of the industry. You simply lead the culture and make sure the organization is edging closer and closer towards the vision. If the organization is not moving in a forward direction, your job is to work to create a more effective and empowering system.

Sure, leaders must be people who understand how to "get into the weeds" when they need to. Great leaders are not above the details. In fact, systems thinking requires understanding the details of the system. However, a leader must not remain in the weeds. Get down into the weeds when necessary and then immediately get back to the birds eye view, making sure the entire system is working properly.

Empower others to do the work for which you hired them for.

This is the mindset of the empowering leader. Allowing other people to be shine and thrive in their roles. Providing guidance when necessary, but allowing others to do the work for which they were hired, for which they are passionate.

# MINDSET OF COACHING

If you were to do a quick Google search of "How To Be A Great Football Coach" or "How To Be A Great Basketball Coach," you would come up with with hundreds, even thousands, of articles on what it takes to be a great coach. Go even deeper and research, "How To Be A Great Business or Executive Coach" and you will find article after article with twenty to thirty bullet points on what it takes to be a great business coach.

However, while all of these traits are meaningful, I believe there are only three mandatory character traits all great coaches must have: (1) knowledge of the game, (2) teaching ability and (3) patience.

When you study the greatest sports coaches of our time, you will see these three traits in every coach. And just to clarify, when I say "patience," I do not mean a patient demeanor. Some of the greatest coaches in any sport are people who are passionate, even hot-headed. When I say patience, I mean the ability to look at a player, to see where they could be and to help them realize their full potential over time. Again, we are talking about mindset here, not necessarily the outer actions of a coach.

Let's dive in a little deeper.

First, the Empowering Leader must understand "the game." Whatever industry the leader finds themselves, he or she must have a deep understanding of that industry. It is true that leadership skills transcend industry. Meaning that a great leader is a great leader no matter the industry or organization. You can place a truly great leader in any company or industry and they will find a way to bring out the highest potential in the people and the organization. However, great leadership means having deep expertise within a given industry. To the understand the industry – and the organization – inside and out. To understand the technical and political realities and to be able to move within this framework.

Leadership is not simply pie-in-the-sky soft skills. Leadership begins with expertise. The people whom you lead will expect that you know, at the very least, what they know. This knowledge is mandatory.

Now, in an age of technology, it is important that you, as the leader, have the same knowledge of every engineer and technician in your employ? Absolutely not. Remember, we discussed earlier in the book that a leader must view his or her team members as consultants. You, as the leader, are a leader and managers of consultants who all bring their own share of expertise to the proverbial table. You do not need to have the same expertise as each of the "consultants" you lead. However, you must have an understating of what each expert brings to the table and, most importantly, what each expert needs from you in order to succeed. This is paramount.

Even more important is understanding strategy within your industry and you organization. Leadership is being strategic. Being strategic requires understanding how the pieces of the organization work together and understand the trends for your industry.

Leadership is no excuse for ignorance. You are not simply the "Vision Gal" or the "Big Picture Guy." You must have a knowledge and understanding of the game in which you are coaching.

Second, an Empowering Leader must be able to teach "the game." Whatever "game" you are leading, you must be able to pass along the necessary knowledge to those you lead.

Teaching is a crucial element towards being an Empowering Leader. A teacher is someone who gives something valuable they have (knowledge) to others. Giving is one of the most empowering uses of your knowledge. Sharing with others in order that they might reach their highest potential.

I have always believed that teaching and leadership go hand in hand. They are one in the same. You cannot truly be a great teacher without understanding the concepts of leadership. You cannot truly be a great leader without understanding the concepts of teaching. Both teaching and leading share a common trait: They are acts of service; laying down one's life for the sake of benefiting another.

This must be the mindset of any would-be Empowering Leader. We continue to repeat the mantra in this book: Leadership is not about you. Leadership is giving of one's life for the greater good. To see where society should be; to see where people in society can be and to have the courage to act.

Think of the the most influential teacher you have ever had. What was the most important trait that attracted you to this educator?

Without knowing you personally, I can tell you what I know about the most influential teacher you have ever had in your life; they believed in you.

Be that person for those you are privileged to lead. See in them what they cannot see for themselves. Reach deep inside of the people you lead and pull out the greatness that is hidden in all of us.

This is the job of the teacher. This is who you must become.

Third and finally, an Empowering Leader must be patient.

As we stated earlier, the kind of patience we are talking about has much less to do with your actions than your mindset. The mindset of patience is the mindset that states, "I take the long view."

I take the long view with my team members.

I take the long view with my employees.

I take the long view with my clients.

I take the long view with my students.

59

I take the long view with my players.

I take the long view with my community.

I take the long view with my patients.

I take the long view with my children.

I take the long view with my spouse.

The long view is this: To see where a person could be and to hold on until you see that person become all they are meant to be.

It is easy to take the short view. To only see what is in front of you right now and to react solely based on the present. The patient leader sees everything and everyone for what they could be and they refuse to give up until the organization, the community, or the person becomes the highest version of themselves.

This is patience.

Your actions may show frustration. Your actions may show disappointment. Your actions may show passion. Your actions may even demonstrate impatience from time to time.

However, your mindset is patience. The people you lead know they can trust you because they know you are not going to give up on them. The organization you lead can trust you because they know you are not going anywhere. Your family can trust you because they know you will consistently be there through thick and through thin.

This is patience.

To remain. To persist. To see the vision. To never let up. To always and only take the long view.

The mindset of coaching is not an easy mindset.

It is easier to keep the knowledge you have to yourself. It is easier to simply tell people what to do rather than to teach them. It easier to use and discard people than it is to demonstrate patience over a long period of time.

One final point on coaching. Coaches are always looking for ways to get better. Coaches are always looking for ways their people can get better. When the team loses, the coach is looking for ways to get better. When the team wins, the coach is still looking for ways for the team to get better. Win or lose, the coach keeps his mindset on the fundamentals and how the overall team can improve. In a sense, the coach is always looking forward, never looking back. At the time of the first printing of this book, Bill Belichick is widely known as one of the greatest professional football coaches in the modern era. After a recent Super Bowl win during the post-game conference, in talking about the win, Belichick stated, "As great as tonight was, we are now five weeks behind for the next season." This is what we call the relentless pursuit of looking forward to the next win.

This is the job of a coach. To seek ways to get better. To consistently keep one's eye towards the vision. To keep looking forward. Let others celebrate. You keep pushing forward.

Be the coach your people need. Take a coach's mindset. If they are winning, it's on them. If they are losing, it's on you to adjust your coaching. Keep your eye on the vision. Bring the best out in your people. Bring the best out in your organization.

---

This is the mindset of the Empowering Leader. To love your people. To be open. To focus on the system. To keep your eyes on the purpose and vision. To coach your people.

## IMPORTANT TAKEAWAYS

- Leadership and love go hand in hand. To love is to "seek the highest good for the other."
- Leadership is never about you. Never. If you need to make life about you, choose another avenue. Leadership is not for you.
- Hire great people. Hire "consultants." Hire experts. Then be open to their feedback. Empower them (give your power to them) to run your organization.
- Long-term success – or failure – is caused by the system, not the people. If your organization is succeeding – or failing – look at the system.
- Understanding the Leadership Matrix is key to becoming an Empowering Leader.

- o Purpose and Oversight is the role of the Board.
- o Vision and Systems Thinking is the role of the Leadership Team
- o Mission and Systems Implementation is the role of the Management Team
- o Innovation and Creation is the role of the Team Members
- o Leadership is teaching. Teaching is leadership.
- o Patience is taking long view with communities, organizations, families, teams and people.

# THE ACTIONS OF THE THE EMPOWERING LEADER

We have discussed the Heart of the Empowering Leader, those aspects which are foundational to the life of a leader. We have discussed the Mindset of the the Empowering Leader, how a would-be empowering should think.

We now turn our attention to the Actions of an Empowering Leader.

Having the right heart or the right mindset mean very little if a leader does not follow up with the right actions.

What I hope to propose in this section of the book is a formula for being an Empowering Leader; a system, if you will. I believe that if you were to do the following seven actions, you will be an Empowering Leader. These are the principles for empowering leadership. These four actions are the rules by which you must guide yourself. If you do these four actions, I will guarantee you will be bring the greatest potential from your people and your organization.

These actions are the following:

- **COMMUNICATE**: Communicate Purpose, Communicate Vision, Communicate Values

- **ENROLL**: Enroll the Right Members for theTeam. Enable These Team Members to Set the Mission. Resource Generously. Discard the Rest.
- **CULTIVATE**: Cultivate a Culture of Ruthless Feedback, Consistent Accountability and Meaningful Rewards. Make Culture Your Number One Priority.
- **EVOLVE**: Be Authentic. Make Continuous Improvements.

When your leadership is defined by these four actions, you will be an Empowering Leader.

Let's dive in.

# COMMUNICATE

In any relationship, communication is key.

Look at any successful – or unsuccessful – relationship and you will see a foundation of great or poor communication. When two or more people are involved, communication is a must.

The job of the leader is to communicate. To communicate Purpose. To communicate Vision. To Communicate Values.

One of the key problems in many organizations is a lack of alignment around a shared purpose, vision and mission. Organizations will hire different people from different backgrounds with different values and different goals and expect these different people to coalesce around a shared vision. It's not going to happen.

The leader must understand (and embody) the purpose, vision and values, hire people who understand (and embody) the purpose, vision and values and then continually communicate the purpose, vision and values of the organization.

Why?

To bring organizational alignment around the purpose (why you exist), vision (where you are going) and values (what you care about).

You will never have a successful organization when you have every person within your organization running in different directions. Everyone must be running in the same direction at the same pace towards the same goals.

I think back to my days in the United States Army. At least once a week, we would do "company runs." Fewer times we would do battalion, brigade and, once, a divisional run. The runs would encompass anywhere from 100 to 10,000 (for the divisional runs) men and women running in-step, in formation and all sounding off to the cadence. For a civilian, what a sight to see! Adult men and women of all ages, different backgrounds and different ethnicities running in alignment towards the same direction.

What kept all of these men and women running in the same direction? Communication.

Before these massive runs would even begin, massive communication would begin. In the days and weeks leading up to the run, we would begin to hear about these runs. We would hear about the importance of the run and what we must do in order to help the company be successful in the run. On the morning of the run, we would gather in formation and hear the details of the run... and why the run was so important. During the run, we run to the motivating sounds of cadence. In one accord, we would all sound off together. After the run, we stand in formation and, once again, hear the how important that run was and how great we did.

The communication served one purpose: to bring alignment.

The Empowering Leader understands the importance of alignment, not for the sake of alignment, but for the sake of the purpose, vision and mission. The Empowering Leader understands that the success of the individual person is dependent on the success of the organization. And vice versa. In order to lead this kind of success, there must be alignment.

Again, we come back to the importance of the Constitution. While the individual must have have a Personal Constitution, the organization must have its own Constitution, a written document with its stated purpose, vision, mission, values and principles. Every decision within the organization must be made in alignment with this Constitution. Every person hired must be in alignment with this Constitution. In order to maintain this alignment throughout time, communication is key.

Because the Empowering Leaders wants the organization to win, he or she will be consistently communicating the purpose, the vision, the mission, the values and the principles. In every meeting, every conversation, every planning session, every coaching session... communicate the Constitution.

# ENROLL

The Empowering Leader understands the importance of attracting and recruiting the right people in order to accomplish the vision and mission of the organization. This may be one of the most important aspects of being a great leader... enrolling the right people to your team, enabling these team members to set the vision, resourcing your team members generously, holding your team accountable for the results and letting go of those team members who are not able to get the job done.

Let's go deeper on this idea of enrolling.

## ENROLL THE RIGHT TEAM MEMBERS

Getting the right people on your team can be one of the most challenging tasks you will face as a leader. Whether you are looking for paid or volunteer team members, this part of being a leader should be a major focus of your time leading.

However, even before choosing team leaders, it is important that you, as the leader, understand the purpose, vision, mission, values and principles of organization and the team. Your recruitment to the team will be 100 percent based on this constitution . The culture you form will be based on this Constitution. It is your responsibility, as the leader, to ensure the people who join your team line up with the constitution. Sure, at times, you will make a mistake in recruiting someone to your team. People will lie. People will act differently in order to be what they think you want them to be. People will withhold their true selves from you. However, time tells all things.

Within 90 to 180 days, you will have an idea of who the new team member is and what they are all about. At this point you, give them full empowerment or release them from the team.

Yet, more often than not, you will bring the right person to your team if you are patient, if you seek advisement and if you enroll the members of the team in the hiring process.

This might be one of the most empowering actions a leader can take. To enroll the current team members in the process of recruiting and accepting newer team members. This will ensure that whatever culture you have built will be sustained. Now, if you desire to change the culture, you must put forth a new Constitution, hold to the values and principles and recruit people to the team who share these same values and will hold to the new principles. Changing the team culture is a another beast altogether. It can be done with the right leader, time and patience.

Unless you are the only member of the team, if at all possible, do not bring new team members to the team without the input of the other team members. This is a recipe for disaster. Always seek advice. Always gain the feedback from the team around you. Leaders who add people to their team using only their viewpoint and experience set up the team where every member of the team is only loyal to the boss. The attitude of every team member at the table is, "There is only one person in this room responsible for my job, position and salary. Therefore, there is only person here I need to have on my side." Of course, your team members will not say this out loud. However, unconsciously their behaviors will showcase this mentality. You will see politics in the worst kind as everyone vies for your attention and approval. They do not need each other; they only need you.

This is not the work of an Empowering Leader. The Empowering Leader does everything he or she can to make sure the team – and the people on the team – are not dependent on him or her. Leaders who want and need every person and every decision dependent on them show personal insecurity. They strive to keep all of the power in their hands as opposed to giving it away. Holding onto power ensures the insecure leader remains in a position where he or she is needed and the team or organization remains dependent on him or her. This is the opposite of empowering. Again, the Empowering Leader is consistently striving to give leadership away to the people and organizations he or she leads.

Enrolling the *right* team members is key. In order to enroll the right team members, you must have trust. You must trust your team members and they must trust you. Trust is key. If you do not believe you will be able to trust your team member, do not bring them on to the team. Trust your gut on this. Trust your team's input on this one. Trust is key. If you would not trust the potential team member with your family or your money, do not bring them into your team. I don't care how great they perform. I don't care what skills they have. If you cannot trust them, the lack of trust will destroy your team and, ultimately, your leadership.

Understanding that you cannot know everything is the key to enrolling the right team members. Again, unless you are the only member of the team, enlist other team members to help you enroll other members of the team. Involving your team members ensures the continuity of the culture of your team and requires the new team members to become dependent on and interdependent with the current members of the team.

Trust is key. However, trust must exist within the group, not simply between the leader and the separate team members. Enrolling the right team members is one of the most important jobs of the Empowering Leader.

## ENABLE YOUR TEAM

Once you have enrolled the right members of the team, the next steps become much easier.

First, you must enable your team to set the mission for the team or the organization.

In larger organizations and corporations, the founder and board set and maintain the purpose for the organization. The leadership team is then responsible for the vision and systems thinking. Management is responsible for setting and achieving the mission in order to achieve the overall purpose. In smaller organizations, the owner or director of the company may find themselves in a dual role of being the board and the executive leadership team. It is important to understand that no matter how small your organization may be, the roles of the Board, Leadership, Management and Team members must be filled. If you are a solo entrepreneur, you may fill each of these roles in the early days, but each role must be filled. As your organization grows, the importance of becoming an Empowering Leader begins to take shape. While you may still be responsible for the purpose (why your organization exists) and the vision (where your organization is going), you must enable your team members to set the mission (how you will reach the vision) for the organization or the team.

What do I mean by this?

No micromanaging.

As an Empowering Leader, you remain focused on the Purpose and ensure that everyone understands why the organization exists. As an Empowering Leader, you remain focused on knowing and communicating the Vision to the rest of the organization. You are consistently reminding the organization, "This is where we are going!"

How you reach the destination should be of no concern to you. You let your team members decide this. You can provide guidance if they need or request your expertise, but you must remain free of the mission. The mission is the job of the team.

Yet, remaining free of the mission is one of the hardest aspects of being a leader. Nearly impossible, if we are honest. Why? Because by our very nature, leaders are "Get the Job Done" kind of people. As leaders, we know what we want and we know how we want it done. Even more, if you are the kind of leader who has remained with one team, one organization, or one mission over a long period of time, more than likely you have either founded or built aspects of said team, organization or mission. You understand the nuts and the bolts of the organization. You understand how to get the job done. It is hard for you to separate yourself from the mission of the organization because you were the original missionary! You alone understand the mission more than anyone else!

However, if you are to be an Empowering Leader, you must remove yourself from the mission. You must enable – and empower – your team to set the mission. Your concern is reaching the destination, the Vision. This is all you care about. How you reach the Vision? Who cares.

And, may I pass along a little word of advice? Stop. Feeling. Guilty.

Stop feeling guilty about the fact that, as an Empowering Leader, you get to do fun work. You have worked hard to get here. You do not have to be involved with the details as much as you once were. Sure, there will be times when you will be called to be in the details. Those times when you need to step in and help guide your team. However, after providing your brief guidance, once again remove yourself and elevate yourself back to the role of the Empowering Leader – focusing on the Purpose and the Vision.

What if you are currently in a management role? Be empowering there! As the manager, communicate the Purpose and Vision that has been communicated to you and then work *with* your team to set the mission. If your mindset is right, this is a very exciting place for you to be. You get to work alongside your team to help accomplish the mission for the organization. You get to be in the weeds with your team members. You get to develop meaningful relationships with your team members. You get to celebrate with your team when you win and work directly with your team when the result does not go as planned. This is a very exciting time for you on your journey to gaining more experience as you move towards the senior leadership role.

The point really is this: Be empowering wherever you are. Give away as much power as you possibly can for the purpose of helping other reach their full and highest potential in life and leadership. Remember, leadership is not about *you*.

## RESOURCE YOUR TEAM

Give your team all of the necessary tools and resources they need in order to succeed.

Again, communicate the Purpose and Vision. Provide them the charge of putting forth the Mission in order to achieve the Purpose and Vision.
Ask them what they need to achieve the mission and, within the best of your ability, give them the resources they need in which to succeed. It could be money. It could be time. It could be people. It could be guidance. It could be literature. It could be training. It could be travel. It could be research. It could be a myriad of resources. Only your team knows what they need in order to succeed.

Because you trust them, you must listen to them. Because you trust them, you have no problem handing over resources from the organization. You know these resources are going to be used for the Purpose, Vision and Mission of the organization. Therefore, to the extent you can, give your team exactly what they need in order to succeed.

Leaders who demand their people achieve the Purpose, Vision and Mission yet do not resource their people towards the Purpose, Vision and Mission are simply setting up their people – and ultimately – the organization for failure. Give your people everything they need in order to succeed.

If you are not able to provide all of the resources your team needs, be the resource they need. Help them in any way they need. This is the time when you must be involved in the mission. You take the role of consultant to your team and be what the team needs you to be.

Never demand from your team what you as the leader are unwilling to resource. At times, you may need to help your team be creative with the resources they have been given, but only demand from them the level of resources you are willing to give them.

Understand this: Resourcing your people does not simply mean giving them the work tools they need in order to succeed. Resourcing your team requires that you resource them as people, as human beings. Pay your people well. Provide over-the-top benefits. Provide all the vacation time they need. When they are sick, give them all the time they need. When their families are sick, give them all the time they need. Give your people as many holidays off as you can. Take your team to lunch of or dinner. Provide Christmas bonuses, if you can. Whatever you can give to your team members, give it to them as often as you can.

The point is this: In every way you can, take care of your team. Resource your team members personally and professionally.

Again, you cannot demand from your people what you are not willing to resource to them.

Resource your people generously in any and every way you can and they will achieve the mission for you in ways you could have never imagined.

# MUTUAL ACCOUNTABILITY FOR RESULTS

Results are key. You will win as a leader if you can consistently lead your team towards effective results. You will grow in confidence and your team's confidence in you will grow the more wins you provide for the team. However, as you know, results do not simply happen on their own. You, as the leader, must drive your team towards these results.

How? Through consistent accountability.

In its basic form, accountability is simply holding each other responsible for the commitments you have made to the team purpose, vision, mission and the team. As a leader, it is up to you to hold your team responsible to achieve the objectives you have set out to achieve. Please understand what I am saying here: As the leader, you must hold the *team* accountable for results.

What you may be thinking I am saying is that it is your team who does the work while you simply stand back and hold everyone accountable. In other words, you remain above the fray, above the work and above the accountability. After all, as the leader you will be held responsible by your supervisor or the board of directors.

This is what the majority of leaders do.

This is not the action of an Empowering Leader.

The Empowering Leader places himself or herself squarely within the realm of feedback, allowing members of the team to provide feedback on how the leader is doing. In other words, as an Empowering Leader, you hold the *team* accountable while allowing each team member to hold other team members accountable...including you. You hold ultimate responsibility for the success of the team while also being held accountable to the team.

Mutual accountability will require a shift in mindset for you. More than anything, mutual accountability will require the attitude and presence of humility on your part.

You are the leader. You understand the purpose, vision and mission. You have been placed in a leadership position because you have shown the ability to understand and achieve the mission better than others. If you are the founder of the company or organization, you have done the work of the team members who sit before you. It may be difficult for you to accept feedback from the very team members who work for you. However, greater emphasis is placed on the team when you submit yourself to accountability by the team. Most importantly, you will grow as a leader when you open yourself to the feedback from your team. Because we all have blindspots, your team will help you discover your blindspots and work to overcome yours. Again, this will require humility on your part.

As an Empowering Leader, holding your team accountable for results is one of the most empowering actions you can take.

Yet, only hold your team responsible for the results...not the process. When leaders begin to get involved in the process, they become much more disempowering. You move from empowering to micromanaging. Unless you are in a field where certain processes must be followed in order to produce effective work, allow your team members to have control over their own process. Leave the process to them; hold the team accountable for the results.

## HIRE SLOW, FIRE FAST

Two of the hardest decisions you will make when leading your team and organization are hiring people and firing people.

Most of the time, you will hire based on the purpose, vision and mission. Most of the time, you will fire based on the culture of the organization.

When hiring, what is the most important question you, as the leader, will ask? "Is this the best person to help us accomplish the purpose, vision and mission?" If the answer is, "Yes," you will hire the person. When firing, the realization that usually happens is, "This person is not performing well individually or with the team." Statistics show that over 70% of the time, when a person is let go from an organization, it is usually an issue with organizational culture or chemistry with others on the team. Most people are not performing so badly they cannot be corrected. Too many times, organizations hire people who simply do not "play well with others."

The old adage was "Hire Fast, Fire Slow." In other words, get people in as quickly as possible and assimilate them to purpose, vision and mission. If they do not work out, give it time. Give more chances. Give opportunities for the person to succeed. Give extra training. Provide coaching. If the person is not playing well with others, provide interventions and counseling. Do whatever it takes to keep people with the organization.

After all, it costs a great deal of time and money to hire somebody new. The mindset becomes like the old Luther Vandross song, "If you can't be with the one you love, love the one your with."

However, a work relationship is not a marriage or lifelong commitment. A work relationship is solely based on purpose, vision, mission, values and principles. To keep someone around your organization who does not line up to the Constitution will actually cost you more in the long run. Morale will decline. Motivation will be lost. Good people will jump ship.

The Empowering Leader always places the purpose, vision, mission, values and principles first. Always. Therefore, the Empowering Leader, who strives for wisdom understands the importance of hiring slow and firing fast.

What do I mean by this?

Take your time when hiring.

Have a hiring process in place that allows you to discover those people who best fit your organizational constitution (purpose, vision, mission, values and principles). Involve several members of the team in the hiring process. Combine as many personality tests into the process in order to gain a better understanding of who the person is. Intentionally make sure the process takes several weeks, even months, to complete. Do whatever it takes to ensure you onboard the right person for the team from the very beginning, ensuring success for the individual and for the team.

If, after a period of time, you discover the person you hired is not working out for any reason, let them go immediately. Be generous and empowering in the separation, but let the person go quickly. Letting a person go from the organization is the most empowering action you take for the person and the organization. Personally speaking, in the times I have been let go from jobs, it was always for the best...for me and for the organization. Even when it hurt or was painful in the moment, looking back, I know it was the best thing.

Remember this: No one ever gets fired from a job they are truly designed for. If a person is struggling to do the job, the position is not meant for them. If a person is struggling to assimilate to the culture, the position is not meant for them. In the heat of the moment, the team member being let go will rarely be able to see this. However you, as the Empowering Leader, must be able to see what is best for the person, the team and the organization.

Be ruthlessly truthful when hiring. Be ruthlessly truthful when firing. Again, both of these actions will be tough. Both actions – hiring and firing – will win you friends and enemies. However, for the Empowering Leader, decisions always come back to the purpose, vision, mission, values and principles. When every decision is made based on these, you will make wise hiring – and firing – decisions.

# CULTIVATE

Culture is everything.

You've heard the famous business saying, "Culture eats strategy for breakfast." Notice the originator of this quote did not say "lunch" or "dinner." No, the quote says "breakfast," the first meal of the day. I think this was intentional.

Culture is everything and culture must come first. You can have all of the strategy, systems and processes in place. You can hire every consultant. You take every training possible. You can attend every conference. None of this will matter one iota if you do not handle the culture of your team or organization.

The Empowering Leader knows and understands this.

To be clear, let's define culture.

Culture how is a way of life for a group of people. By culture we mean how a group "does things." Beliefs, behaviors, attitudes, goals, values, morals and customs... each of these components come together to create what we know as culture.

The root word for "culture" is "cult." In our modern age, the word "cult" has a very dark connotation for us. We think of religious groups that live deep in the woods, far away from the world. Groups that shun larger society for their own customs, traditions and ways of life. Often, this kind of cult behavior has caused deep pain for the members of the group and society at large. Yet, a "cult," in it basic form, is a society of people who share the same foundational beliefs and actions.

This being the case, your own family is a cult. There are certain practices and norms that you have established in your family and others practices and norms that are not acceptable within your cult. The same could be said for the schools and churches you attended. If you were on a good sports team, you were part of a "cult." In its basic form a "cult" is neither good or bad; it just is. Every group, team, family, organization and community have a culture, where it is intentional or not. This being the case, it would be wise for the leader to be intentional about creating the desired culture from the ground up.

How?

The Personal or Organizational Constitution.

By now, I am sure you have come to see how important this Constitution is. Understanding your organization and team's purpose, vision, mission, values and principles – and hiring people who align with these – is the key to a strong culture within your organization.

I cannot stress this enough: Culture must come first.

As an Empowering Leader, this must be your highest priority. Why? You cannot give power away within a dysfunctional culture. Giving power away is the goal of every Empowering Leader. In order to give power away, there must be trust.

More than likely you have experienced a toxic culture at some point in your life. Either in a relationship, family or organization. The signs are the same in all three: Fear, lack of motivation, lack of engagement, lack of trust, gossip, resentment, jealousy, sabotage, high turnover, workforce anxiety and more. I know I have worked for my shared of toxic organizations, as I am sure you have as well. You know there can be no empowerment within this kind of culture. The leader must first fix the culture, before giving power away.

We understand the importance of the Constitution (Purpose, Vision, Mission, Values and Principles). These must come first. However, in addition to the Constitution, I would like to offer you three additional concepts to help you grow a dynamic and effective culture: Ruthless Feedback, Consistent Team-Based Accountability and Meaningful Rewards.

## RUTHLESS FEEDBACK

We all have blindspots. You have blindspots. I have blindspots.

Blindspots are those areas in our lives that we cannot see because, more often than not, we do not know these blindspots exist. The areas could be a myriad of issues: Failing to listen to others, interrupting others, gossiping too much, being consistently late, exhibiting a bad attitude, having a lazy work ethic, being negative and many more behaviors. Often, because we have become accustomed to our own behaviors, we do not know how we are perceived by others. This is especially true if you have been successful in your professional career. Because of your success, you may have a difficult time understanding those areas where you need personal work. The answer to this problem is feedback.

Often in organizations, everyone sees everyone else's flaws. As you know, people are very liberal in talking about these flaws to everyone... except for the person with the flaw! But here is the question to ponder as you think about your own flaws: If everyone in the organization is discussing your flaws to everyone but you, how will you get better? The reality is you will not get better until you receive the feedback from those who can see your flaws clearly. Being able to receive this kind of feedback requires two principles within the work environment. First, the culture must be one where everyone is expected to give feedback to others directly, privately and within the context of the team. Second, the culture must be one where everyone is expected to receive feedback from others, privately and within the context of the team.

When you can lead this kind of culture, you are on your way to creating an organization where true innovation and creation can take place. What holds back so many organizations from achieving this true innovation and creativity? The lack of honesty with others.

When team members cannot be honest with each other, they hold back their true feelings and frustrations. This frustration begins to well up over time causing personal issues within the organization that will hold the organization back from achieving its purpose, vision and mission. Too often we take the feelings of the people in our organizations and teams for granted. We do not appreciate or value them. We fail to understand the impact of emotions on the bottom line for the organization. The way to control the emotions for the organization is to bring them surface. Force them to the surface.

As the Empowering Leader, force ruthless feedback within your organization and team. This, of course, requires that you provide and receive ruthless feedback first. In a very practical sense, at the end of the meetings you lead, do not end your meeting until you have gone around the room and asked everyone for feedback on the meeting and your leadership within the meeting. Ask for everyone's feedback on ideas shared, how they are feelings about the ideas shared, what they would change and what could be improved. Give time for everyone to share their ideas or concerns. Make it clear that "back room conversations" are not tolerated but that each team member has full power to share anything and everything they need to share within the meeting. In addition, make it clear that within your team culture, every team member must be ready to hear ruthless feedback for the purpose of making each other better.

The highest potential for any team or person can only be reached through ruthless feedback. The Empowering Leader seeks to help his or her team members not only be successful for the organization; the Empower Leader seeks to help his or her team members reach their highest potential in life. This potential can only be reached through true and ruthless feedback; giving ruthless and empowering feedback and receiving ruthless and empowering feedback from the senior leader to the most junior team member.

## CONSISTENT TEAM-BASED ACCOUNTABILITY

To be accountable for something is to be responsible for that something. A commitment has been made by an individual, team or organization and now the work must be accomplished. And while responsibility can be achieved by one person, accountability takes two or more people. Accountability rarely happens well within the company of one. The accountability may be between partners, from board to senior leadership, from senior leadership to management or management to the direct line team members. However, accountability looks, it is an agreement between two or more parties to ensure the person or team who made the commitment holds to that commitment.

Yet, for the Empowering Leader, accountability is much more than simply "being the boss." The Empowering Leader consistently looks for ways to give power away. When it comes to accountability, the Empowering Leader places the power squarely within the hands of the team. Team members are no longer accountable to one person. Team members are accountable to – and for – each other.

Team-based accountability goes back to the idea of a culture of ruthless and empowering feedback. Every member of the team or organization is subject to honest and straightforward feedback from any other member of the team, especially those team members who are closest to the leader, manager or team member.

What I am advocating for is a move from the top-down leadership model to towards a team-based leadership model. While the the leader of the organization or team is ultimately responsible for the success or failure of the team, the power rests within the team and not simply one person within the team.

What are the benefits of team-based accountability?

First, with team-based accountability, you empower your people. As with any team organization, you lead some very strong and gifted people. Some of these people are imagining theirselves in your position one day. This is a good thing. Again, because leadership is all about putting first the purpose, vision, mission, values and principles of the organization, the Empowering Leader understands the mission of the organization must come before personal desires of the leader. In a very basic sense, human nature is very protective and seeks to eliminate any outside threats. This protective nature leads to personal jealousy and insecurity within the life of a would-be leader causing him or her to remove any person they view as threat to their position. This mindset is completely against the nature of the Empowering Leader. The Empowering Leader always places personal feelings aside and seeks to give as much power away thereby empowering his or her people. Team members who feel fully empowered will be much more fulfilled and effective in accomplishing the mission.

Second, with team-based accountability, you give every member of your team a voice. Again, because you are leading some strong and dynamic people, they need a voice in the mission and the process. Giving a voice to every member of your team is one of the most empowering actions any leader can take. Every member of your team has an opinion on everything. Even the quieter members of your team... they have an opinion! However, because they may feel dominated by other members of the team, they may not speak up as clearly or as often. Team-based accountability gives voice to every member of the team because everyone on the team is accountable to every other member of the team. The team will move in a cohesive way when each team member feels their voice – and their opinion – is valued.

Finally, with team-based accountability, you lessen your influence on the mission. As a strong leader, your default leadership style could very well be autocratic; you alone hold the power to determine the vision and mission of the organization. This leadership style works well in organizations or cultures where people do not want responsibility; cultures where people respond best to being told what to do. In Western-based organizations, giving more power away to your team members is the way to success. Less of you, more of the team. Again, your "job" as the leader is to simply make sure the team is on purpose, moving towards the vision and is in tact with the values and principles of the organization. The mission – where the real work happens – is not up to you. Remove yourself as often as you can and watch your team flourish and reach their highest potential in creativity and innovation.

As a leader, it will be hard to move towards team-based accountability. Every fiber in you will want to hold onto control. However, you are an Empowering Leader. It is never about you.

## MEANINGFUL REWARDS

Reward your people. Celebrate the successes of your people.

80

When it comes to parenting or teaching children, you have probably heard the saying, "Praise in public; punish in private." This is simply great leadership.

Allow the accountability and team-based decision making to happen behind closed doors. However, when your team succeeds – and they will – shout these successes from the mountaintops. Reward your team. Celebrate them and celebrate with them.

Most importantly, celebrate in ways that are meaningful to them, not you. Must I repeat it? Leadership is not about you.

Creating meaningful rewards may mean that you reward your team members in different ways. However, as a group, ask your team how they want to be rewarded. Before you begin a project, simply ask the question: "Team, if we accomplish this goal, how are we going to reward ourselves?" Then, you as the leader, get to make that happen.

Whatever you do, make sure to reward your team. Disempowering Leaders consistently harp on the negative aspects of their team. Empowering Leaders drive their teams toward excellence and then celebrate along the way.

Reward your team.

I cannot stress this enough. Culture is everything.

As the leader in your organization, you must make culture you number one priority. Are you on purpose? What is the vision? Are you moving towards the vision? What is the mission? Are your team members accomplishing the mission alone goals they have set? What are your organizational values (belief) and principles (rules)? Are you recruiting people based on these values and principles?

This is your primary focus as the leader. Cultivating your organization. Cultivating your team. Cultivating your people.

When people leave your organization, the Empowering Leader wants people to be able to say, "I am better for having worked there."

The choice is up to you.

# EVOLVE

The Empowering Leader is an evolving leader.

Commitment to personal growth is an essential trait of being an Empowering Leader. Being authentic, being open to feedback and making continuous improvements in life and leadership. These actions are key to be an empowering leader.

We have talked about the importance of feedback so we will not belabor the point. Yet, feedback is worth very little if there is no action to change based on the feedback received.

The question is, "Does one simply evolve automatically?" If so, how? If not, what does it take to evolve.

To answer the questions, yes, everyone does evolve automatically...in some ways. All of us start as little little versions of ourselves. However, over time, we grow up. Our bodies physically grow and expand. We become taller. We become bigger. Through training and education, we grow in our understanding of the world works and how to interact with others in more mature ways. We develop self-restraint. We learn the importance of getting along to go along.

Yes, there is a certain amount of automatic evolution based on our society and context. Most of this evolution falls within the realm of, what I call, outer evolution. We change because we have to. Scientifically, we must evolve and, for survival, the environment we are in forces us to evolve.

However, for the Empowering Leader, the outer evolution is not the primary focus. The inner evolution is where the work takes place. The inner evolution is the growth and progress of the mental, emotional and spiritual aspects of ones life. These aspects do evolve automatically. We all know someone who continues to grow older and evolve physically yet somehow remains stunted mentally, emotionally and spiritually. We call these people "immature" because they have not fully matured. The reality is that many people remain "immature" throughout their lives; some just hide it more than others.

For the Empowering Leader, immaturity is not an option. The Empowering Leader seeks to be firing on all cylinders physically, mentally, emotionally and spiritually. This maturity and growth requires evolution.

In order to evolve, you must (1) reflect, (2) expand your knowledge and (3) experiment with new things. This is process of evolution, which is the process of mastery. As we shared in the beginning of this book, mastery is key to being a high effective and empowering leader.

## REFLECT

To reflect is to look back into one's history in order to make one's future even better. There can be no personal evolution without personal reflection.

In order to be an Empowering Leader, you must be a person who takes seriously the power of reflection.

Reflection can happen in many different formats, but the format I strongly recommend is the written word. To sit down and write longhand or type out your thoughts on a piece of paper. As you probably know, there is something powerful and freeing that happens when thoughts are untangled on paper. There are people who prefer to reflect through dialogue. These are verbal processors. While verbal processing is certainly a way to reflect, writing out your own thoughts in your own journal and in your own company is truly the best way come to grips with your life, your choices and your progress.

Reflection is all about progress. Moving forward. Looking back in order to move forward.

This being the case, you must know and understand your Personal Constitution. Your Personal Constitution is the direction you are moving towards in life. Reflecting on your history without having a plan for the future is simply looking back. While there is nothing wrong with looking back simply for the sake of looking back, as an Empowering Leader you are consistently working to evolve and remain relevant. In order to remain relevant, you must keep your eyes squarely focused on the future.

So sit down and write. Write often.

At the very least, you must reflect once a year. However, I would say reflecting once a year will yield very little, if any, rewards for your leadership. Just like going to gym once a year would provide little to no benefit to your life, so it is with reflection. I would counter and recommend reflecting briefly every day. Just as you want to work out and eat healthy every day you also want to create empowering habits that will help you reach your goal on a daily basis. You can reflect in the morning or the evening. It is simply important that you make reflection a daily practice, a normal part of your daily routine.

If daily reflection does not work with your schedule, you must make time to reflect once a week, preferably at the end of each week. You will not reach your goals if you are not making time to reflect on a regular basis.

To go even deeper, make consistent time for the team you lead to reflect. To look back in order to go forward. Just as you must consistently be evolving, so must your team be consistently evolving in order to remain relevant.

What is involved in your reflection? Purposeful reflection requires looking at your Personal Constitution, line by line, and reflecting on it. Are you living on purpose? Are you working towards your vision? Are you accomplishing your mission on a daily and weekly basis? Are you holding true to your values? Are you living according to your principles? If not, why not? These are the topics you can include in your intentional reflection.

Evolution and remaining relevant are aspects of the Empowering Leader. Evolution and remaining relevant are only possible with intentional and empowering reflection.

## EXPAND

Evolution involves expanding your mind. Opening up yourself to what is different and what is new.

In politics, you have heard of the terms conservative and progressive. The term "conservative" typically refers to the desire to hold on to the past, to conserve history. The term "progressive" typically refers to the desire to look into the future, to progress in a forward movement. In this manner, evolution is progressive term. The reality is this: life is always moving forward. Always.

Society is always moving forward. On a geopolitical scale, as the cultures and races continue to move and immigrate across the world, the world is expanding. Certain areas of the world once known for a certain race and culture are currently in the process of forming new histories as new people and new ways of living slowly descend on certain regions around the world. We see these trends happening in larger scales within areas of Europe and North America. The world is changing. The world is becoming smaller, more flat. The internet is helping to create a world of greater opportunity where anyone with access to the internet, an entrepreneurial spirit and the willingness to work hard has the ability to create opportunity. Where once it took a person hours, even days, to access information, this same person can access information within minutes and seconds.

The world is expanding. You can progress forward or you can work to conserve the past, the way the world used to be.

The Empowering Leader embraces the world and seeks to expand their own horizons. In a very real way, the Empowering Leader is faced with diversity within his or her team and organization as the global changes become present within the team. The Empowering Leader embraces people and changes and seeks to give power away to anyone who helps to achieve the personal or organizational constitution.

The constitution – personal or organizational – is the only litmus test for the truly Empowering Leader. The only question the Empowering Leader cares about is this, "Can this person help me and this team achieve our Constitution?" This is the only litmus test.

Religion does not matter. Personal beliefs do not matter. Personal Creed does not matter. Race does not matter. Sexual orientation does not matter. Color does not matter. Gender does not matter. Marital status does not matter. Age does not matter.

For the Empowering Leader, all that matters is the Purpose, Vision, Mission, Values and Principles of the organization. This being the case, the Empowering Leader seeks to expand his or her mind to new ways of thinking and new ways of living. This intentional expansion of the mind is one of the primary drivers of growth and evolution within a leader.

The world is constantly evolving. So must you.

# EXPERIMENT

There can be no evolution without experimentation. I would argue experimentation is evolution.

If you desire to evolve as a leader, as a team or as an organization, you must consistently be experimenting with new things and new ideas. Discovery, which leads to evolution, begins with experimenting.

It starts in the mind. You or a member of your team think of an idea, a hypothesis, something you would like to do with the team or organization. From here, you decide to test the idea within a controlled environment. A controlled environment is key. By "control," we mean this: The hypothesis must fit within the Constitution of the organization. For example, if you lead a hamburger restaurant that only serves hamburgers and a member of your team hypothesizes about selling electronics to help increase the bottom line, more than likely you would agree, as a team, to not follow through on this experimentation. Why? You sell hamburgers. The experimentation you would be seeking, within a hamburger restaurant, is how to improve your hamburgers, how to market your restaurant better and how to increase the quality of customer service. The experimentation would fall within the purpose, vision, mission, values and principles of your organization. However, within this "control" all bets are off. No idea is turned away on how to improve burgers, marketing or the customer service experience. Until you discover the perfect formula, you continue to experiment with new ideas. No new idea is cut off. Nothing is shut down.

You experiment. You allow your team members to experiment. And you repeat the experimentation process until, again, you discover the perfect formula for your team or business.

The Disempowering Leader runs from experimentation because they are running from change. More than likely, the Disempowering Leader has discovered a system that work for him or her. Change within that already developed system requires change within the leader. And, as we know, change is hard.

Yet, consistent change, development and growth must be at the heart of the Empowering Leader. Life never remains still. You must never remain still.

Experimentation within your team or organization allows your team members the freedom to grow and expand within their own work and leadership. Closing yourself and your organization off to experimentation puts a damper on the people who look to you for vision, leadership, guidance and the *permission* to grow and expand. Much like placing a container over a candle extinguishes the fire quickly due to a lack of oxygen, so does a disempowering leader's actions toward the motivation and desire to create and innovate within the team member.

Experimentation is key to evolution. Experiment consistently. Allow your people to consistently experiment. Experiment until you discover the the most effective formula for your organization.

Evolve... and release your people into their full and highest potential.

Empowering Leadership begins in the Heart and moves towards the mind. However, leadership is not empowering if not expressed in the actions of the leader. To believe something and to think something is not the same as doing. Empowering Leadership is not a noun, it is a verb. Leadership that gives power away in tangle and effective ways.

# IMPORTANT TAKEAWAYS

- Organizational alignment happens as a result of constant communication.
- Enrolling right team members is not solely to job the leader. The team must be involved in hiring the right person into the organization.
- The Empowering Leader communicates purpose and vision to team but remains free of the mission.
- You cannot expect from your team what you are not willing to resource to them.
- Resourcing your team means taking care of the team member professionally and personally. Be as generous as you can be with your team members.
- The Empowering Leader is accountable for and *to* the team.
- Hire slow and fire fast. Never make quick decisions when hiring a member of your team.

- For the Empowering Leader, culture is everything. The majority of focus for the Empowering Leader is on building and maintaining the culture of the team.
- The organizational Constitution is the primary driver for culture within your team or organization.
- The Empowering Leader is always in the process of evolving personally and professionally. The world is evolving; so must you.

# WHY IT MATTERS

From the age 18 until 65-70, men and women around the globe give their lives to corporations, companies, institutions and organizations, all in the name of progressing our world forward. These men and women give up personal hopes, dreams, rest and family time in order to help industry succeed on a global scale.

Because of this sacrifice that takes place on a global scale every day, leaders and organizations must hold up their end of the bargain with the people who give so much to make these organizations work. It is the responsibility of the leaders and managers to empower the people who work hard to produce profit, impact and effectiveness for global industry. It is the responsibility for ever leader and manager to help every team member to use their 40-50 years in the workforce to reach their personal potential while also helping the organization reach maximum effectiveness.

Leadership is not for the weak or the selfish. Leadership is the calling for the person who seeks to help others be the highest and best version of themselves.

Your leadership matters because the people you lead matter.

Period. End of story.

# ABOUT J.C. HURTADO-PRATER

J.C. Hurtado-Prater has extensive nonprofit executive experience and now serves as a leadership consultant, speaker, and principal for Cannonball Consulting, a leadership training and coaching company.

A community leader in the South Bay of San Diego County, Hurtado-Prater serves as the worship pastor for New Hope Community Church, a church that impacts over 2,000 people on a weekly basis. J.C. is a member of the Chancellor's Community Advisory Board for UC San Diego and board of directors for both South Bay Community Services and the Southwestern College Foundation. J.C. sits on bond oversight committees for the city of Chula Vista, Southwestern College and the Chula Vista Elementary School District. In addition, J.C. gives motivational speeches to hundreds of local youth each year as a member of the Los Angeles Chargers outreach team.

A veteran of the United States Army, J.C. received his bachelor of arts from UCLA, his master in business administration from Saint Joseph's College of Maine and is currently pursuing his doctoral degree in Education Policy, Organization and Leadership through the University of Illinois at Urbana-Champaign.

J.C. is passionate about one thing: empowering people and organizations to achieve their highest potential in life and leadership.

For speaking or training, you can email JC directly at jc@jchp.co

# NOTES

# NOTES

# NOTES

# NOTES

# NOTES

# NOTES

# NOTES

# NOTES

# NOTES

# NOTES

# NOTES